Table of Contents

THE ULTIMATE NINJA FOODI AIR FRYER UK COOKBOOK FOR BEGINNERS

1000 No-fuss, fast and Delicious Recipes incl.Side Dishes, Desserts and More.|Full Color Pictures Version

KARI B. ROSEBERRY

Introduction

I like to think of my Ninja Foodi air fryer as the appliance of all appliances. Since I got my first one, I have had little use for all other appliances in my home. Except for liquids like chai, I can prepare almost any other meal with my Ninja Foodi.

It has proven to be a versatile appliance that serves me in almost anything I desire to eat. Whether I am craving a quick snack or I need to prepare a complete evening meal for the whole family, my trusty Ninja Foodi air fryer has never let me down.

If you just got your Ninja Foodi air fryer and did not know what to cook with it, this cookbook will be an eye-opener. I have spent many hours working on these recipes to perfect them. They can be scaled up for the whole family or made for one person. You will find many creative uses for ingredients you are already familiar with at your local food market.

HOW DOES IT WORK

Understanding how the Ninja Foodi air fryer works will speed up the learning curve when making delicious meals. Like other air fryers, the Ninja Foodi uses circulating hot air to mimic the deep-frying process without all the excessive oil.

What makes it stand out is that it comes with two baskets. You can use them for cooking different foods simultaneously. One unique feature is the Smart Finish, which lets you sync the frying process, ensuring both are ready at the same time. It has a large capacity, which means you can make up to 4 pounds of French fries or chicken.

To get the most out of it, arrange your ingredients in an even layer at the bottom. Ensure that the ingredients do not overlap. However, if you are preparing large quantities, pause the cooking halfway, and shake the basket. It ensures that everything will cook evenly.

If you love eating dehydrated fruit, ensure that you only have a single layer of ingredients during cooking. A rack is placed on top of them, followed by a new layer of ingredients. It will ensure that everything is evenly dehydrated.

CLEANING THE AIR FRYER

Once you are done cooking, unplug the air fryer to clean it. Once done, wipe down the exterior and control panel using a damp cloth. Never immerse the main unit in water. All the detachable plates and baskets are dishwasher friendly. Alternatively, you can clean them in the sink with soap and water. According to Ninja, hand washing will help extend the life of the detachable.

If there is sticky food residue on the baskets, and plates, soak them in warm water with soap. It helps preserve the life of the inserts.

You must read the instruction booklet before using the Ninja Foodi air fryer. It comes with clear diagrams and instructions on how to use the various functions of this air fryer. Most of these functions are intuitive, and you will get them in the first hour of handling the appliance.

With your Ninja Foodi air fryer, you are now part of a new experience involving quick, delicious, healthy meals.

An air fryer is a small appliance that uses circulating hot air and a small amount of oil to cook food. It is a healthier alternative to traditional deep frying, as it uses less oil and produces food with fewer calories and less fat. Air fryers are typically easy to use and clean, and can be a convenient and versatile option for home cooks.

Air Frying Overview

Choosing the right air fryer: There are many different models and sizes of air fryers on the market, so it is important to choose the right one for your needs. Consider factors such as size, capacity, features, and price to find an air fryer that is suitable for your cooking needs.

Preparing the food: Before air frying, make sure to cut the food into small, even-sized pieces and season as desired. Use a cooking spray or brush to lightly coat the food with oil. This will help to ensure that the food cooks evenly and has a crispy and flavorful texture.

Setting the temperature and time: Different foods require different temperature and cooking time settings in order to cook properly. Make sure to follow the instructions in the manual or the recipe to determine the appropriate

temperature and cooking time for the food you are cooking. Some air fryers also have pre-set cooking programs for common foods, such as chicken or fries.

Cleaning the air fryer: After cooking, make sure to clean the air fryer according to the instructions in the manual. This will help to maintain the performance of the air fryer and ensure that it is ready for your next cooking adventure.

MILLARD EFFECT

The Millard effect is a phenomenon in which the texture and mouthfeel of food is improved by adding a small amount of fat or oil. The effect is named after the French chemist Louis-Camille Maillard, who first described the chemical reactions between amino acids and sugars that produce the flavors and colors of cooked food. The Millard effect is commonly used in air frying, where a small amount of oil is added to the food to improve its texture and flavor.

HOW TO ACHIEVE BETTER MILLARD EFFECT

To achieve a better Millard effect when air frying, there are several steps you can take. Here are some possible ways to improve the texture and flavor of air fried food:

Use a light coating of oil: Before air frying, lightly coat the food with a small amount of oil using a cooking spray or brush. This will help to ensure that the oil is evenly distributed on the surface of the food, and will provide the necessary moisture and flavor for the Millard effect.

Season the food: In addition to oil, seasonings and spices can also enhance the flavor of air fried food. Try experimenting with different herbs and spices to add depth and complexity to the flavor of the food.

Preheat the air fryer: Some air fryers require preheating before cooking. Make sure to follow the instructions in the manual for preheating your air fryer, as this can help to improve the texture and flavor of the food.

Use the right cooking time and temperature: Different foods require different cooking time and temperature settings to achieve the best results. Make sure to follow the instructions in the manual or the recipe to determine the appropriate settings for the food you are cooking.

Use Air Fryers to Prepare Ingredients

There are many scenarios where you can use an air fryer to prepare ingredients for cooking. Here are a few examples of how you can use an air fryer to prepare ingredients:

Pre-cooking meats: Air fryers can be used to pre-cook meats, such as chicken breasts or pork chops, before adding them to a recipe. This can help to partially cook the meat, which can reduce the overall cooking time and ensure that the meat is cooked evenly and to the desired level of doneness.

Pre-browning vegetables: Air fryers can be used to pre-brown vegetables, such as onions or mushrooms, before adding them to a recipe. This can help to enhance the flavor and texture of the vegetables, and can also add depth and complexity to the overall dish.

Pre-baking crusts: Air fryers can be used to pre-bake pie or quiche crusts, which can help to create a crispy and flaky texture. This can be particularly useful when making crusts that are prone to becoming soggy or undercooked, such as gluten-free or whole wheat crusts.

Tips for Better Air Frying

PREPARING TO AIR-FRY

Here are some tips for preparing to air fry:

Read the instructions in the manual: Before air frying, make sure to read the instructions in the manual for your air fryer. This will provide important information on how to use the air fryer safely and effectively, and will also include tips on choosing the right temperature and cooking time for different types of food.

Choose the right ingredients: Air fryers are well-suited for a wide variety of ingredients, but some are better suited for air frying than others. Choose ingredients that are dry and have a relatively high fat content, such as chicken breasts or potatoes, for the best results. Avoid wet or saucy ingredients, such as soups or stews, as these may not cook evenly in an air fryer.

Cut the ingredients into small, even-sized pieces: To ensure that the food cooks evenly in the air fryer, make sure to cut the ingredients into small, even-sized pieces. This will help to ensure that the food cooks at the same rate, and will also make it easier to turn the food and check for doneness.

Use a light coating of oil: To achieve the best texture and flavor when air frying, use a light coating of oil or cooking spray on the ingredients. This will help to add moisture and flavor to the food, and will also promote the development of the Millard effect, which can improve the texture and mouthfeel of the food.

WHILE YOU ARE AIR-FRYING

Use a cooking spray or brush to add oil: If the food is starting to dry out or stick to the bottom of the air fryer, use a cooking spray or brush to add a small amount of oil. This will help to add moisture and flavor to the food, and will also promote the development of the Millard effect, which can improve the texture and mouthfeel of the food.

Turn the food regularly: To ensure that the food cooks evenly, make sure to turn the food regularly while it is cooking in the air fryer. Use a fork or tongs to carefully flip the food, and make sure to turn the food evenly to avoid tearing or breaking apart.

Check the food for doneness: To avoid overcooking or burning the food, make sure to check on the food regularly while it is cooking in the air fryer. Use a fork or tongs to poke the food and check for doneness, and remove the food from the air fryer when it is cooked to your desired level of doneness.

Use a digital thermometer to check the internal temperature: If you are unsure whether the food is cooked to the appropriate level of doneness, use a digital thermometer to check the internal temperature of the food. Different foods require different internal temperatures to ensure that they are safe to eat, so make sure to consult a cooking chart or recipe to determine the appropriate temperature for the food you are cooking.

AFTER YOU AIR-FRY

Here are some tips for after you have finished air frying:

Let the food rest: After removing the food from the air fryer, let it rest for a few minutes before serving. This will allow the food to continue cooking and will also allow the juices to redistribute, which can improve the flavor and texture of the food.

Serve the food immediately: Air fried food is best served immediately after it is cooked, as it can lose its crispness and texture over time. Make sure to serve the food as soon as it is ready, and avoid letting it sit for too long before serving.

Season the food: If desired, season the food with salt, pepper, or other seasonings after air frying. This can help to enhance the flavor of the food and make it more satisfying.

Clean the air fryer: After air frying, make sure to clean the air fryer according to the instructions in the manual. This will help to maintain the performance of the air fryer and ensure that it is ready for your next cooking adventure.

Chapter 2
Breads & Breakfast

Indian Masala Omelet

Prep Time: 10 minutes | Cook Time: 12 minutes | Serves 2

- 4 large eggs
- ½ cup diced onion
- ½ cup diced tomato
- ¼ cup chopped fresh cilantro
- 1 jalapeño, seeded and finely chopped
- ½ teaspoon ground turmeric
- ½ teaspoon kosher salt
- ½ teaspoon cayenne pepper
- Olive oil for greasing the pan

1. In a large bowl, beat the eggs. Stir in the onion, tomato, cilantro, jalapeño, turmeric, salt, and cayenne.
2. Generously grease a 3-cup Bundt pan. (Be sure to grease the pan well—the proteins in eggs stick something fierce. And do not use a round baking pan. The hole in the center of a Bundt pan allows hot air to circulate through the middle of the omelet so that it will cook at the same rate as the outside.)
3. Pour the egg mixture into the prepared pan. Place the pan in the air fryer basket. Set the air fryer to 250°F for 12 minutes, or until the eggs are cooked through. Carefully unmold and cut the omelet into four pieces (2 pieces per serving).

Frico (Cheese Crisps)

Prep Time: 10 minutes | Cook Time: 5 minutes | Serves 2

- 1 cup shredded or grated aged Manchego cheese
- 1 teaspoon all-purpose flour
- ½ teaspoon cumin seeds
- ¼ teaspoon cracked black pepper

1. Line the air-fryer basket with a round of parchment paper cut to fit.
2. In a small bowl, toss together the cheese and flour. Sprinkle the cheese in a 4 to 4½-inch round in the center of the parchment-lined air-fryer basket. In a small bowl, stir together the cumin seeds and pepper. Sprinkle the spices on top of the cheese.
3. Set the air fryer to 375°F for 5 minutes. After 4 minutes, check for doneness: The cheese should be bubbling and just starting to darken a bit. If not, cook for 1 minute more. Use a thin, flexible metal spatula to transfer the cheese wafer to a paper towel–lined baking sheet to cool (it will continue to crisp up as it cools).
4. While the cheese wafer is still warm, cut it into wedges and let cool completely. Serve the cheese wafers, or store between layers of waxed paper or parchment paper in an airtight container at room temperature for up to 5 days.

Quiche Cups

Prep Time: 15 minutes | Cook Time: 26 minutes | Serves 10 quiche cups

- ¼ pound all-natural ground pork sausage
- 3 eggs
- ¾ cup milk
- 20 foil muffin cups
- cooking spray
- 4 ounces sharp Cheddar cheese, grated

1. Divide sausage into 3 portions and shape each into a thin patty.
2. Place patties in air fryer basket and cook 390°F for 6 minutes.
3. While sausage is cooking, prepare the egg mixture. A large measuring cup or bowl with a pouring lip works best. Combine the eggs and milk and whisk until well blended. Set aside.
4. When sausage has cooked fully, remove patties from basket, drain well, and use a fork to crumble the meat into small pieces.
5. Double the foil cups into 10 sets. Remove paper liners from the top muffin cups and spray the foil cups lightly with cooking spray.
6. Divide crumbled sausage among the 10 muffin cup sets.
7. Top each with grated cheese, divided evenly among the cups.
8. Place 5 cups in air fryer basket.
9. Pour egg mixture into each cup, filling until each cup is at least ⅔ full.
10. Cook for 8 minutes and test for doneness. A knife inserted into the center shouldn't have any raw egg on it when removed.
11. If needed, cook 1 to 2 more minutes, until egg completely sets.
12. Repeat steps 8 through 11 for the remaining quiches.

Cran-Bran Muffins

Prep Time: 15 minutes | Cook Time: 15 minutes | Serves 8 muffins

- 1½ cups bran cereal flakes
- 1 cup plus 2 tablespoons whole-wheat pastry flour
- 3 tablespoons packed brown sugar
- 1 teaspoon low-sodium baking powder
- 1 cup 2 percent milk
- 3 tablespoons safflower oil or peanut oil
- 1 egg
- ½ cup dried cranberries

1. In a medium bowl, mix the cereal, pastry flour, brown sugar, and baking powder.
2. In a small bowl, whisk the milk, oil, and egg until combined.
3. Stir the egg mixture into the dry ingredients until just combined (see Tip).
4. Stir in the cranberries.
5. Double up 16 foil muffin cups to make 8 cups. Put 4 cups into the air fryer and fill each three-fourths full with batter. Bake for about 15 minutes, or until the muffin tops spring back when lightly touched with your finger.
6. Repeat with the remaining muffin cups and batter.
7. Let cool on a wire rack for 10 minutes before serving.

Dried Fruit Beignets

Prep Time: 22 minutes | Cook Time: 8 minutes | Serves 16

- 1 teaspoon active quick-rising dry yeast
- ⅓ cup buttermilk
- 3 tablespoons packed brown sugar
- 1 egg
- 1½ cups whole-wheat pastry flour
- 3 tablespoons chopped dried cherries
- 3 tablespoons chopped golden raisins
- 2 tablespoons unsalted butter, melted
- Powdered sugar, for dusting (optional)

1. In a medium bowl, mix the yeast with 3 tablespoons of water. Let it stand for 5 minutes, or until it bubbles.
2. Stir in the buttermilk, brown sugar, and egg until well mixed.
3. Stir in the pastry flour until combined.
4. With your hands, work the cherries and raisins into the dough. Let the mixture stand for 15 minutes.
5. Pat the dough into an 8-by-8-inch square and cut into 16 pieces. Gently shape each piece into a ball.
6. Drizzle the balls with the melted butter. Place them in a single layer in the air fryer basket so they don't touch. You may have to cook these in batches. Air-fry for 5 to 8 minutes, or until puffy and golden brown.
7. Dust with powdered sugar before serving, if desired.

Sausage Egg Muffins

Prep Time: 10 minutes | Cook Time: 20 minutes | Serves 4

- 6 oz Italian sausage
- 6 eggs
- 1/8 cup heavy cream
- 3 oz cheese

1. Preheat the fryer to 350°F/175°C.
2. Grease a muffin pan.
3. Slice the sausage links and place them two to a tin.
4. Beat the eggs with the cream and season with salt and pepper.
5. Pour over the sausages in the tin.
6. Sprinkle with cheese and the remaining egg mixture.
7. Cook for 20 minutes or until the eggs are done and serve!

Spinach-Bacon Rollups

Prep Time: 5 minutes | Cook Time: 9 minutes | Serves 4

- 4 flour tortillas (6- or 7-inch size)
- 4 slices Swiss cheese
- 1 cup baby spinach leaves
- 4 slices turkey bacon

1. Preheat air fryer to 390°F.
2. On each tortilla, place one slice of cheese and ¼ cup of spinach.
3. Roll up tortillas and wrap each with a strip of bacon. Secure each end with a toothpick.
4. Place rollups in air fryer basket, leaving a little space in between them.
5. Cook for 4 minutes. Turn and rearrange rollups (for more even cooking) and cook for 4 to 5 minutes longer, until bacon is crisp.

Black's Bangin' Casserole

Prep Time: 5 minutes | Cook Time: 35 minutes | Serves 4

- 5 eggs
- 3 tbsp chunky tomato sauce
- 2 tbsp heavy cream
- 2 tbsp grated parmesan cheese

1. Preheat your fryer to 350°F/175°C.
2. Combine the eggs and cream in a bowl.
3. Mix in the tomato sauce and add the cheese.
4. Spread into a glass baking dish and bake for 25-35 minutes.
5. Top with extra cheese.
6. Enjoy!

Scrambled Mug Eggs

Prep Time: 3 minutes | Cook Time: 2 minutes | Serves 1

- 1 mug
- 2 eggs
- Salt and pepper
- Shredded cheese
- Your favorite buffalo wing sauce

1. Crack the eggs into a mug and whisk until blended.
2. Put the mug into your microwave and cook for 1.5 – 2 minutes, depending on the power of your microwave.
3. Leave for a few minutes and remove from the microwave.
4. Sprinkle with salt and pepper. Add your desired amount of cheese on top.
5. Using a fork, mix everything together.
6. Then add your favorite buffalo or hot sauce and mix again.
7. Serve!

Puff Pastry Bites with Goat Cheese, Figs & Prosciutto

Prep Time: 30 minutes | Cook Time: 10 minutes | Serves 8

- 2 slices prosciutto
- ½ cup soft goat cheese
- 4 dried Mission figs, chopped
- 2 teaspoons snipped fresh tarragon or basil
- 1 large egg
- 1 tablespoon water
- All-purpose flour
- 1 sheet frozen puff pastry (from a 17.3-ounce package), thawed

1. Place the prosciutto slices on a paper towel. Lay another towel on top. Microwave on high for 1 minute. Remove the top paper towel and let cool completely (the meat will be slightly flexible but will crisp up as it cools). Crumble the prosciutto; set aside.
2. In a medium bowl, stir together the goat cheese, figs, crisped prosciutto, and tarragon until well blended.
3. In a small bowl, beat the egg and water with a fork to make an egg wash. Lightly flour a work surface. Roll out the thawed puff pastry sheet to a 12-inch square. Using a pizza cutter, cut the pastry into sixteen 3-inch squares. Brush the edges of the squares with the egg wash.
4. Place about 2 teaspoons of the goat cheese mixture in the center of each square. Fold the pastry over the filling to form triangles, pressing the edges to seal. Crimp the edges with a fork.
5. Arrange 8 of the pastry triangles in the air-fryer basket, leaving as much space as possible between them. Set the air fryer to 400°F for 10 minutes, or until the pastry is golden brown. Transfer the finished pastries to a serving plate and repeat with the remaining pastry triangles.
6. Serve warm.

Cranberry Beignets

Prep Time: 15 minutes | Cook Time: 10 minutes | Serves 16 beignets

- 1½ cups flour
- 2 teaspoons baking soda
- ¼ teaspoon salt
- 3 tablespoons brown sugar
- ⅓ cup chopped dried cranberries
- ½ cup buttermilk
- 1 egg
- 3 tablespoons melted unsalted butter

1. In a medium bowl, combine the flour, baking soda, salt, and brown sugar, and mix well. Stir in dried cranberries.
2. In a small bowl, combine the buttermilk and egg, and beat until smooth. Stir into the dry ingredients just until moistened.
3. Pat the dough into an 8-by-8-inch square and cut into 16 pieces. Coat each piece lightly with melted butter.
4. Place in a single layer in the air fryer basket, making sure the pieces don't touch. You may have to cook in batches depending on the size of your air fryer basket. Air-fry for 5 to 8 minutes or until puffy and golden brown. Dust with powdered sugar before serving, if desired.

Scotch Eggs

Prep Time: 10 minutes | Cook Time: 25 minutes | Serves 4

- 2 tablespoons flour, plus extra for coating
- 1 pound ground breakfast sausage
- 4 hardboiled eggs, peeled
- 1 raw egg
- 1 tablespoon water
- oil for misting or cooking spray
- ¾ cup panko breadcrumbs
- ¾ cup flour

1. Combine flour with ground sausage and mix thoroughly.
2. Divide into 4 equal portions and mold each around a hardboiled egg so the sausage completely covers the egg.
3. In a small bowl, beat together the raw egg and water.
4. Dip sausage-covered eggs in the remaining flour, then the egg mixture, then roll in the crumb coating.
5. Cook at 360°F for 10 minutes. Spray eggs, turn, and spray other side.
6. Continue cooking for another 10 to 15 minutes or until sausage is well done.

Strawberry Rhubarb Parfait

Prep Time: 1-2 days | Cook Time: 0 minutes | Serves 1

- 1 package crème fraiche or plain full-fat yogurt (8.5 oz)
- 2 tbsp toasted flakes
- 2 tbsp toasted coconut flakes
- 6 tbsp homemade strawberry and rhubarb jam (4.25 oz)

1. Add the jam into a dessert bowl (3 tbsp per serving).
2. Add the crème fraîche and garnish with the toasted and coconut flakes.
3. Serve!

Dutch Pancake

Prep Time: 12 minutes | Cook Time: 15 minutes | Serves 4

- 2 (scant) tablespoons unsalted butter
- 3 eggs
- ½ cup flour
- ½ cup milk
- ½ teaspoon vanilla
- 1½ cups sliced fresh strawberries
- 2 tablespoons powdered sugar

1. Preheat the air fryer with a 6-by-6-by-2-inch pan in the basket. Add the butter and heat until the butter melts.
2. Meanwhile, in a medium bowl, add the eggs, flour, milk, and vanilla, and beat well with an eggbeater until combined and frothy.
3. Carefully remove the basket with the pan from the air fryer and tilt so the butter covers the bottom of the pan. Immediately pour in the batter and put back in the fryer.
4. Bake for 12 to 16 minutes or until the pancake is puffed and golden brown.
5. Remove from the oven; the pancake will fall. Top with strawberries and powdered sugar and serve immediately.

Banana Chia Seed Pudding

Prep Time: 1-2 days | Cook Time: 0 minutes | Serves 1

- 1 can full-fat coconut milk
- 1 medium- or small-sized banana, ripe
- ½ tsp cinnamon
- 1 tsp vanilla extract
- ¼ cup chia seeds

1. In a bowl, mash the banana until soft.
2. Add the remaining ingredients and mix until incorporated.
3. Cover and place in your refrigerator overnight.
4. Serve!

Salmon Omelet

Prep Time: 5 minutes | Cook Time: 40 minutes | Serves 2

- 3 eggs
- 1 smoked salmon
- 3 links pork sausage
- ¼ cup onions
- ¼ cup provolone cheese

1. Whisk the eggs and pour them into a skillet.
2. Follow the standard method for making an omelette.
3. Add the onions, salmon and cheese before turning the omelet over.
4. Sprinkle the omelet with cheese and serve with the sausages on the side.
5. Serve!

Hash Brown

Prep Time: 10 minutes | Cook Time: 10 minutes | Serves 2

- 12 oz grated fresh cauliflower (about ½ a medium-sized head)
- 4 slices bacon, chopped
- 3 oz onion, chopped
- 1 tbsp butter, softened

1. In a skillet, sauté the bacon and onion until brown.
2. Add in the cauliflower and stir until tender and browned.
3. Add the butter steadily as it cooks.
4. Season to taste with salt and pepper.
5. Enjoy!

Chapter 3
Snacks & Appetizers

Curly's Cauliflower

Prep Time: 10 minutes | Cook Time: 20 minutes | Serves 4

- 4 cups bite-sized cauliflower florets
- 1 cup friendly bread crumbs, mixed with 1 tsp. salt
- ¼ cup melted butter [vegan/other]
- ¼ cup buffalo sauce [vegan/other]
- Mayo [vegan/other] or creamy dressing for dipping

1. In a bowl, combine the butter and buffalo sauce to create a creamy paste.
2. Completely cover each floret with the sauce.
3. Coat the florets with the bread crumb mixture. Cook the florets in the Air Fryer for approximately 15 minutes at 350°F, shaking the basket occasionally.
4. Serve with a raw vegetable salad, mayo or creamy dressing.

Fried Mushrooms

Prep Time: 10 minutes | Cook Time: 30 minutes | Serves 4

- 2 lb. button mushrooms
- 3 tbsp. white or French vermouth [optional]
- 1 tbsp. coconut oil
- 2 tsp. herbs of your choice
- ½ tsp. garlic powder

1. Wash and dry the mushrooms. Slice them into quarters.
2. Pre-heat your Air Fryer at 320°F and add the coconut oil, garlic powder, and herbs to the basket.
3. Briefly cook the ingredients for 2 minutes and give them a stir. Put the mushrooms in the air fryer and cook for 25 minutes, stirring occasionally throughout.
4. Pour in the white vermouth and mix. Cook for an additional 5 minutes.
5. Serve hot.

Cheesy Garlic Bread

Prep Time: 10 minutes | Cook Time: 10 minutes | Serves 2

- 1 friendly baguette
- 4 tsp. butter, melted
- 3 chopped garlic cloves
- 5 tsp. sundried tomato pesto
- 1 cup mozzarella cheese, grated

1. Cut your baguette into 5 thick round slices.
2. Add the garlic cloves to the melted butter and brush onto each slice of bread.
3. Spread a teaspoon of sun dried tomato pesto onto each slice.
4. Top each slice with the grated mozzarella.
5. Transfer the bread slices to the Air Fryer and cook them at 180°F for 6 – 8 minutes.
6. Top with some freshly chopped basil leaves, chili flakes and oregano if desired.

Stuffed Mushrooms

Prep Time: 15 minutes | Cook Time: 10 minutes | Serves 4

- 6 small mushrooms
- 1 tbsp. onion, peeled and diced
- 1 tbsp. friendly bread crumbs
- 1 tbsp. olive oil
- 1 tsp. garlic, pureed
- 1 tsp. parsley
- Salt and pepper to taste

1. Combine the bread crumbs, oil, onion, parsley, salt, pepper and garlic in a bowl.
2. Scoop the stalks out of the mushrooms and spoon equal portions of the crumb mixture in the caps. Transfer to the Air Fryer and cook for 10 minutes at 350°F.
3. Serve with mayo dip if desired.

Broccoli

Prep Time: 10 minutes | Cook Time: 20 minutes | Serves 4

- 1 large head broccoli
- ½ lemon, juiced
- 3 cloves garlic, minced
- 1 tbsp. coconut oil
- 1 tbsp. white sesame seeds
- 2 tsp. Maggi sauce or other seasonings to taste

1. Wash and dry the broccoli. Chop it up into small florets.
2. Place the minced garlic in your Air Fryer basket, along with the coconut oil, lemon juice and Maggi sauce.
3. Heat for 2 minutes at 320°F and give it a stir. Put the garlic and broccoli in the basket and cook for another 13 minutes.
4. Top the broccoli with the white sesame seeds and resume cooking for 5 more minutes, ensuring the seeds become nice and toasty.

Granola Three Ways

Prep Time: 10 minutes | Cook Time: 10 minutes | Serves 4

- Nantucket Granola
- ¼ cup maple syrup
- ¼ cup dark brown sugar
- 1 tablespoon butter
- 1 teaspoon vanilla extract
- 1 cup rolled oats
- ½ cup dried cranberries
- ½ cup walnuts, chopped
- ¼ cup pumpkin seeds
- ¼ cup shredded coconut
- Blueberry Delight
- ¼ cup honey
- ¼ cup light brown sugar
- 1 tablespoon butter
- 1 teaspoon lemon extract
- 1 cup rolled oats
- ½ cup sliced almonds
- ½ cup dried blueberries
- ¼ cup pumpkin seeds
- ¼ cup sunflower seeds
- Cherry Black Forest Mix
- ¼ cup honey
- ¼ cup light brown sugar
- 1 tablespoon butter
- 1 teaspoon almond extract
- 1 cup rolled oats
- ½ cup sliced almonds
- ½ cup dried cherries
- ¼ cup shredded coconut
- ¼ cup dark chocolate chips
- oil for misting or cooking spray

1. Combine the syrup or honey, brown sugar, and butter in a small saucepan or microwave-safe bowl. Heat and stir just until butter melts and sugar dissolves. Stir in the extract.
2. Place all other dry ingredients in a large bowl. (For the Cherry Black Forest Mix, don't add the chocolate chips yet.)
3. Pour melted butter mixture over dry ingredients and stir until oat mixture is well coated.
4. Lightly spray a baking pan with oil or cooking spray.
5. Pour granola into pan and cook at 390°F for 5 minutes. Stir. Continue cooking for 2 to 5 minutes, stirring every minute or two, until golden brown. Watch closely. Once the mixture begins to brown, it will cook quickly.
6. Remove granola from pan and spread on wax paper. It will become crispier as it cools.
7. For the Cherry Black Forest Mix, stir in chocolate chips after granola has cooled completely.
8. Store in an airtight container.

Cheesy Zucchini Chips

Prep Time: 5 minutes | Cook Time: 10 minutes | Serves 4

- 1 pound zucchini, sliced
- 1 cup Pecorino Romano cheese, grated
- Sea salt and cayenne pepper, to taste

1. Start by preheating your Air Fryer to 390 degrees F.
2. Toss the zucchini slices with the remaining ingredients and arrange them in a single layer in the Air Fryer cooking basket.
3. Cook the zucchini slices for about 10 minutes at 390 degrees F, shaking the basket halfway through the cooking time. Work in batches.
4. Bon appétit!

Herb Tomato Chips

Prep Time: 5 minutes | Cook Time: 15 minutes | Serves 2

- 1 beefsteak tomato, thinly sliced
- 2 tablespoons extra-virgin olive oil
- Coarse sea salt and fresh ground pepper, to taste
- 1 teaspoon dried basil
- 1 teaspoon dried thyme
- 1 teaspoon dried rosemary

1. Toss the tomato slices with the remaining ingredients until they are well coated on all sides.
2. Arrange the tomato slices in the Air Fryer cooking basket.
3. Cook the tomato slices at 360 degrees F for about 10 minutes. Turn the temperature to 330 degrees F and continue to cook for a further 5 minutes.
4. Bon appétit!

Carrots & Rhubarb

Prep Time: 10 minutes | Cook Time: 25 minutes | Serves 4

- 1 lb. heritage carrots
- 1 lb. rhubarb
- 1 medium orange
- ½ cup walnuts, halved
- 2 tsp. walnut oil
- ½ tsp. sugar or a few drops of sugar extract

1. Rinse the carrots to wash. Dry and chop them into 1-inch pieces.
2. Transfer them to the Air Fryer basket and drizzle over the walnut oil.
3. Cook at 320°F for about 20 minutes.
4. In the meantime, wash the rhubarb and chop it into ½-inch pieces.
5. Coarsely dice the walnuts.
6. Wash the orange and grate its skin into a small bowl. Peel the rest of the orange and cut it up into wedges.
7. Place the rhubarb, walnuts and sugar in the fryer and allow to cook for an additional 5 minutes.
8. Add in 2 tbsp. of the orange zest, along with the orange wedges. Serve immediately.

Grilled Tomatoes

Prep Time: 5 minutes | Cook Time: 20 minutes | Serves 2

- 2 tomatoes, medium to large
- Herbs of your choice, to taste
- Pepper to taste
- High quality cooking spray

1. Wash and dry the tomatoes, before chopping them in half.
2. Lightly spritz them all over with cooking spray.
3. Season each half with herbs (oregano, basil, parsley, rosemary, thyme, sage, etc.) as desired and black pepper.
4. Put the halves in the tray of your Air Fryer. Cook for 20 minutes at 320°F, or longer if necessary. Larger tomatoes will take longer to cook.

Paprika Potato Chips

Prep Time: 4 minutes | Cook Time: 16 minutes | Serves 3

- 1 pound potatoes, thinly sliced
- 2 tablespoons olive oil
- 1 teaspoon paprika
- Coarse salt and cayenne pepper, to taste

1. Start by preheating your Air Fryer to 360 degrees F.
2. Toss the potatoes with the remaining ingredients and place them in the Air Fryer cooking basket.
3. Air fry the potato chips for 16 minutes, shaking the basket halfway through the cooking time and work in batches.
4. Enjoy!

Phyllo Artichoke Triangles

Prep Time: 15 minutes | Cook Time: 9 minutes | Serves 18 triangles

- ¼ cup ricotta cheese
- 1 egg white
- ⅓ cup minced drained artichoke hearts
- 3 tablespoons grated mozzarella cheese
- ½ teaspoon dried thyme
- 6 sheets frozen phyllo dough, thawed
- 2 tablespoons melted butter

1. In a small bowl, combine ricotta cheese, egg white, artichoke hearts, mozzarella cheese, and thyme, and mix well.
2. Cover the phyllo dough with a damp kitchen towel while you work so it doesn't dry out. Using one sheet at a time, place on the work surface and cut into thirds lengthwise.
3. Put about 1½ teaspoons of the filling on each strip at the base. Fold the bottom right-hand tip of phyllo over the filling to meet the other side in a triangle, then continue folding in a triangle. Brush each triangle with butter to seal the edges. Repeat with remaining phyllo dough and filling.
4. Bake, 6 at a time, for about 3 to 4 minutes or until the phyllo is golden brown and crisp.

Roasted Mixed Nuts

Prep Time: 4 minutes | Cook Time: 6 minutes | Serves 4

- 1/4 cup almonds
- 1/2 cup hazelnuts
- 1/4 cup peanuts

1. Preheat your Air Fryer to 330 degrees F.
2. Air fry the nuts for 6 minutes, shaking the basket halfway through the cooking time and working in batches.
3. Enjoy!

Garlic Wings

Prep Time: 1 hour 20 minutes | Cook Time: 15 minutes | Serves 4

- 2 pounds chicken wings
- oil for misting
- cooking spray
- 1 cup buttermilk
- 2 cloves garlic, mashed flat
- 1 teaspoon Worcestershire sauce
- 1 bay leaf
- 1½ cups grated Parmesan cheese
- ¾ cup breadcrumbs
- 1½ tablespoons garlic powder
- ½ teaspoon salt

1. Mix all marinade ingredients together.
2. Remove wing tips (the third joint) and discard or freeze for stock. Cut the remaining wings at the joint and toss them into the marinade, stirring to coat well. Refrigerate for at least an hour but no more than 8 hours.
3. When ready to cook, combine all coating ingredients in a shallow dish.
4. Remove wings from marinade, shaking off excess, and roll in coating mixture. Press coating into wings so that it sticks well. Spray wings with oil.
5. Spray air fryer basket with cooking spray. Place wings in basket in single layer, close but not touching.
6. Cook at 360°F for 13 to 15 minutes or until chicken is done and juices run clear.
7. Repeat previous step to cook remaining wings.

Southwest Stuffed Mushrooms

Prep Time: 15 minutes | Cook Time: 12 minutes | Serves 4

- 16 medium button mushrooms, rinsed and patted dry
- ⅓ cup low-sodium salsa
- 3 garlic cloves, minced
- 1 medium onion, finely chopped
- 1 jalapeño pepper, minced (see Tip)
- ⅛ teaspoon cayenne pepper
- 3 tablespoons shredded pepper Jack cheese
- 2 teaspoons olive oil

1. Remove the stems from the mushrooms and finely chop them, reserving the whole caps.
2. In a medium bowl, mix the salsa, garlic, onion, jalapeño, cayenne, and pepper Jack cheese. Stir in the chopped mushroom stems.
3. Stuff this mixture into the mushroom caps, mounding the filling. Drizzle the olive oil on the mushrooms. Air-fry the mushrooms in the air fryer basket for 8 to 12 minutes, or until the filling is hot and the mushrooms are tender. Serve immediately.

Spinach Dip with Bread Knots

Prep Time: 12 minutes | Cook Time: 21 minutes | Serves 6

- Nonstick cooking spray
- 1 (8-ounce) package cream cheese, cut into cubes
- ¼ cup sour cream
- ½ cup frozen chopped spinach, thawed and drained
- ½ cup grated Swiss cheese
- 2 green onions, chopped
- ½ (11-ounce) can refrigerated breadstick dough
- 2 tablespoons melted butter
- 3 tablespoons grated Parmesan cheese

1. Spray a 6-by-6-by-2-inch pan with nonstick cooking spray.
2. In a medium bowl, combine the cream cheese, sour cream, spinach, Swiss cheese, and green onions, and mix well. Spread into the prepared pan and bake for 8 minutes or until hot.
3. While the dip is baking, unroll six of the breadsticks and cut them in half crosswise to make 12 pieces.
4. Gently stretch each piece of dough and tie into a loose knot; tuck in the ends.
5. When the dip is hot, remove from the air fryer and carefully place each bread knot on top of the dip, covering the surface of the dip. Brush each knot with melted butter and sprinkle Parmesan cheese on top.
6. Bake for 8 to 13 minutes or until the bread knots are golden brown and cooked through.

Garlic-Herb Pita Chips

Prep Time: 5 minutes | Cook Time: 6 minutes | Serves 4

- ¼ teaspoon dried basil
- ¼ teaspoon marjoram
- ¼ teaspoon ground oregano
- ¼ teaspoon garlic powder
- ¼ teaspoon ground thyme
- ¼ teaspoon salt
- 2 whole 6-inch pitas, whole grain or white
- oil for misting or cooking spray

1. Mix all seasonings together.
2. Cut each pita half into 4 wedges. Break apart wedges at the fold.
3. Mist one side of pita wedges with oil. Sprinkle with half of seasoning mix.
4. Turn pita wedges over, mist the other side with oil, and sprinkle with remaining seasonings.
5. Place pita wedges in air fryer basket and cook at 330°F for 2 minutes.
6. Shake basket and cook for 2 minutes longer. Shake again, and if needed cook for 1 or 2 more minutes, until crisp. Watch carefully because at this point they will cook very quickly.

Buffalo Cauliflower Snacks

Prep Time: 15 minutes | Cook Time: 5 minutes | Serves 6

- 1 large head cauliflower, separated into small florets
- 1 tablespoon olive oil
- ½ teaspoon garlic powder
- ⅓ cup low-sodium hot wing sauce
- ⅔ cup nonfat Greek yogurt
- ½ teaspoons Tabasco sauce
- 1 celery stalk, chopped
- 1 tablespoon crumbled blue cheese

1. In a large bowl, toss the cauliflower florets with the olive oil. Sprinkle with the garlic powder and toss again to coat. Put half of the cauliflower in the air fryer basket. Air-fry for 5 to 7 minutes, until the cauliflower is browned, shaking the basket once during cooking.
2. Transfer to a serving bowl and toss with half of the wing sauce. Repeat with the remaining cauliflower and wing sauce.
3. In a small bowl, stir together the yogurt, Tabasco sauce, celery, and blue cheese. Serve with the cauliflower for dipping.

Arancini

Prep Time: 15 minutes | Cook Time: 22 minutes | Serves 16 aracini

- 2 cups cooked and cooled rice or leftover risotto
- 2 eggs, beaten
- 1½ cups panko bread crumbs, divided
- ½ cup grated Parmesan cheese
- 2 tablespoons minced fresh basil
- 16 ¾-inch cubes mozzarella cheese
- 2 tablespoons olive oil

1. In a medium bowl, combine the rice, eggs, ½ cup of the bread crumbs, Parmesan cheese, and basil. Form this mixture into 16 1½-inch balls.
2. Poke a hole in each of the balls with your finger and insert a mozzarella cube. Form the rice mixture firmly around the cheese.
3. On a shallow plate, combine the remaining 1 cup bread crumbs with the olive oil and mix well. Roll the rice balls in the bread crumbs to coat.
4. Cook the arancini in batches for 8 to 11 minutes or until golden brown.

Pepperoni Pizza Bites

Prep Time: 12 minutes | Cook Time: 16 minutes | Serves 8

- ½ cup (2 ounces) pepperoni (very finely chopped)
- 1 cup finely shredded mozzarella cheese
- ¼ cup Marinara Sauce or store-bought variety
- 1 (8-ounce) can crescent roll dough
- All-purpose flour, for dusting

1. In a small bowl, toss together the pepperoni and cheese. Stir in the marinara sauce. (If you have one, this is a good time to use a food processor. Then you don't have to chop everything so fine; just dump everything in and pulse a few times to mix.)
2. Unroll the dough onto a lightly floured cutting board. Separate it into 4 rectangles. Firmly pinch the perforations together and pat or roll the dough pieces flat.
3. Divide the cheese mixture evenly between the rectangles and spread it out over the dough, leaving a ¼-inch border. Roll a rectangle up tightly, starting with the short end. Pinch the edge down to seal the roll. Repeat with the remaining rolls. If you have time, refrigerate or freeze the rolls for 5 to 10 minutes to firm up. This makes slicing easier.
4. Slice the rolls into 4 or 5 even slices. Place the slices on the sheet pan, leaving a few inches between each.
5. Select AIR ROAST, set temperature to 350°F, and set time to 12 minutes. Select START/PAUSE to begin preheating.
6. Once the unit has preheated, slide the pan into the oven.
7. After 6 minutes, rotate the pan 180 degrees and continue cooking.
8. When cooking is complete, the rolls will be golden brown with crisp edges. Remove the pan from the oven. If you like, serve with additional marinara sauce for dipping.

Mini Tuna Melts with Scallions and Capers

Prep Time: 12 minutes | Cook Time: 6 minutes | Serves 6

- 2 (5- to 6-ounce) cans oil-packed tuna, drained
- 1 small stalk celery, chopped
- 1 large scallion, chopped
- ⅓ cup mayonnaise, or more to taste
- 1 tablespoon capers, drained
- ¼ teaspoon celery salt (optional)
- 1 tablespoon chopped fresh dill (optional)
- 12 slices cocktail rye bread
- 2 tablespoons butter, melted
- 6 slices sharp cheddar or Swiss-style cheese (about 3 ounces)

1. In a medium bowl, mix together the tuna, celery, scallion, mayonnaise, capers, celery salt, and dill (if using).
2. Brush one side of the bread slices with the butter. Arrange the bread slices on the pan, buttered-sides down. Scoop a heaping tablespoon of the tuna mixture on each slice of bread, spreading it out evenly to the edges.
3. Cut the cheese slices to fit the dimensions of the bread and place a cheese slice on each piece.
4. Select AIR ROAST, set temperature to 375°F, and set time to 6 minutes. Select START/PAUSE to begin preheating.
5. Once the unit has preheated, slide the pan into the oven.
6. After 4 minutes, remove the pan from the oven and check the tuna melts. They usually take at least 5 minutes, but depending on the cheese you're using and the temperature of the tuna salad, it can take anywhere from 4 to 6 minutes. The tuna melts are done when the cheese has melted and the tuna is heated through. If needed, continue cooking.
7. When cooking is complete, remove the pan from the oven. Use a spatula to transfer the tuna melts to a cutting board and slice each one in half diagonally (this will make them easier to eat). Serve warm.

Hawaiian Chicken with Pineapple

Prep Time: 5 minutes | Cook Time: 30 minutes | Serves 4

- 1 pound chicken legs, boneless
- Kosher salt and freshly ground black pepper, to taste
- 2 tablespoons tamari sauce
- 1 tablespoon hot sauce
- 1 cup pineapple, peeled and diced
- 1 tablespoon fresh cilantro, roughly chopped

1. Pat the chicken dry with paper towels. Toss the chicken legs with the salt, black pepper, tamari sauce, and hot sauce.
2. Cook the chicken at 380 degrees F for 30 minutes, turning them over halfway through the cooking time.
3. Top the chicken with the pineapple and continue to cook for 5 minutes more. Serve warm, garnished with the fresh cilantro.
4. Bon appétit!

Authentic Chicken Fajitas

Prep Time: 5 minutes | Cook Time: 30 minutes | Serves 4

- 1 pound chicken legs, boneless, skinless, cut into pieces
- 2 tablespoons canola oil
- 1 red bell pepper, sliced
- 1 yellow bell pepper, sliced
- 1 jalapeno pepper, sliced
- 1 onion, sliced
- 1/2 teaspoon onion powder
- 1/2 teaspoon garlic powder
- Sea salt and ground black pepper, to taste

1. Pat the chicken dry with paper towels. Toss the chicken legs with 1 tablespoon of the canola oil.
2. Cook the chicken at 380 degrees F for 15 minutes, shaking the basket halfway through the cooking time.
3. Add the remaining ingredients to the Air Fryer basket and turn the heat to 400 degrees F. Let it cook for 15 minutes more or until cooked through.
4. Bon appétit!

Marinated Turkey Wings

Prep Time: 4 minutes plus marinating time | Cook Time: 40 minutes | Serves 5

- 2 pounds turkey wings, bone-in
- 2 garlic cloves, minced
- 1 small onion, chopped
- 1 tablespoon Dijon mustard
- 1/2 cup red wine
- Sea salt and ground black pepper, to taste
- 1 teaspoon poultry seasoning

1. Place the turkey wings, garlic, onion, mustard, and wine in a ceramic bowl. Cover the bowl and let the turkey marinate in your refrigerator overnight.
2. Discard the marinade and toss the turkey wings with the salt, black pepper, and poultry seasoning.
3. Cook the turkey wings at 400 degrees F for 40 minutes, turning them over halfway through the cooking time.
4. Bon appétit!

Chicken Breasts & Spiced Tomatoes

Prep Time: 10 minutes | Cook Time: 30 minutes | Serves 1

- 1 lb. boneless chicken breast
- Salt and pepper
- 1 cup butter
- 1 cup tomatoes, diced
- 1 ½ tsp. paprika
- 1 tsp. pumpkin pie spices

1. Preheat your fryer at 375°F.
2. Cut the chicken into relatively thick slices and put them in the fryer. Sprinkle with salt and pepper to taste. Cook for fifteen minutes.
3. In the meantime, melt the butter in a saucepan over medium heat, before adding the tomatoes, paprika, and pumpkin pie spices. Leave simmering while the chicken finishes cooking.
4. When the chicken is cooked through, place it on a dish and pour the tomato mixture over. Serve hot.

Sweet-and-Spicy Drumsticks with Garlic Green Beans

Prep Time: 5 minutes | Cook Time: 25 minutes | Serves 4

- 8 skin-on chicken drumsticks
- 1 teaspoon kosher salt or ½ teaspoon fine salt, divided
- 1 pound green beans, trimmed
- 2 garlic cloves, minced
- 2 tablespoons vegetable oil
- ⅓ cup Thai sweet chili sauce

1. Salt the drumsticks on all sides with ½ teaspoon of kosher salt. Let sit for a few minutes, then blot dry with a paper towel. Place on the sheet pan.
2. Select AIR ROAST, set temperature to 375°F, and set time to 25 minutes. Select START/PAUSE to begin preheating.
3. Once preheated, slide the pan into the oven.
4. While the chicken cooks, place the green beans in a large bowl. Add the remaining ½ teaspoon kosher salt, the garlic, and oil. Toss to coat.
5. After 15 minutes, remove the pan from the oven. Brush the drumsticks with the sweet chili sauce. Place the green beans on the pan. Return the pan to the oven and continue cooking.
6. When cooking is complete, the green beans should be sizzling and browned in spots and the chicken cooked through, reading 165°F on a meat thermometer. Serve the chicken with the green beans on the side.

Stir-Fried Chicken with Mixed Fruit

Prep Time: 10 minutes | Cook Time: 15 minutes | Serves 4

- 1 pound low-sodium boneless skinless chicken breasts, cut into 1-inch pieces
- 1 medium red onion, chopped
- 1 (8-ounce) can pineapple chunks, drained, ¼ cup juice reserved
- 1 tablespoon peanut oil or safflower oil
- 1 peach, peeled, pitted, and cubed
- 1 tablespoon cornstarch
- ½ teaspoon ground ginger
- ¼ teaspoon ground allspice
- Brown rice, cooked (optional)

1. In a medium metal bowl, mix the chicken, red onion, pineapple, and peanut oil. Cook in the air fryer for 9 minutes. Remove and stir.
2. Add the peach and return the bowl to the air fryer. Cook for 3 minutes more. Remove and stir again.
3. In a small bowl, whisk the reserved pineapple juice, the cornstarch, ginger, and allspice well. Add to the chicken mixture and stir to combine.
4. Cook for 2 to 3 minutes more, or until the chicken reaches an internal temperature of 165°F on a meat thermometer and the sauce is slightly thickened.
5. Serve immediately over hot cooked brown rice, if desired.R

Chicken Cordon Bleu

Prep Time: 15 minutes | Cook Time: 15 minutes | Serves 4

- 4 chicken breast filets
- ¼ cup chopped ham
- ⅓ cup grated Swiss or Gruyère cheese
- ¼ cup flour
- Pinch salt
- Freshly ground black pepper
- ½ teaspoon dried marjoram
- 1 egg
- 1 cup panko bread crumbs
- Olive oil for misting

1. Put the chicken breast filets on a work surface and gently press them with the palm of your hand to make them a bit thinner. Don't tear the meat.
2. In a small bowl, combine the ham and cheese. Divide this mixture among the chicken filets. Wrap the chicken around the filling to enclose it, using toothpicks to hold the chicken together.
3. In a shallow bowl, mix the flour, salt, pepper, and marjoram. In another bowl, beat the egg. Spread the bread crumbs out on a plate.
4. Dip the chicken into the flour mixture, then into the egg, then into the bread crumbs to coat thoroughly.
5. Put the chicken in the air fryer basket and mist with olive oil.
6. Bake for 13 to 15 minutes or until the chicken is thoroughly cooked to 165°F. Carefully remove the toothpicks and serve.

Ham and Cheese Stuffed Chicken Burgers

Prep Time: 12 minutes | Cook Time: 16 minutes | Serves 4

- ⅓ cup soft bread crumbs
- 3 tablespoons milk
- 1 egg, beaten
- ½ teaspoon dried thyme
- Pinch salt
- Freshly ground black pepper
- 1¼ pounds ground chicken
- ¼ cup finely chopped ham
- ⅓ cup grated Havarti cheese
- Olive oil for misting

1. In a medium bowl, combine the bread crumbs, milk, egg, thyme, salt, and pepper. Add the chicken and mix gently but thoroughly with clean hands.
2. Form the chicken into eight thin patties and place on waxed paper.
3. Top four of the patties with the ham and cheese. Top with remaining four patties and gently press the edges together to seal, so the ham and cheese mixture is in the middle of the burger.
4. Place the burgers in the basket and mist with olive oil. Grill for 13 to 16 minutes or until the chicken is thoroughly cooked to 165°F as measured with a meat thermometer.

Zingy Duck Breast

Prep Time: 5 minutes | Cook Time: 15 minutes | Serves 4

- 2 tablespoons fresh lime juice
- 1 ½ pounds duck breast
- 2 tablespoons olive oil
- 1 teaspoon cayenne pepper
- Kosher salt and freshly ground black pepper, to taste

1. Pat the duck breasts dry with paper towels. Toss the duck breast with the remaining ingredients.
2. Cook the duck breast at 330 degrees F for 15 minutes, turning them over halfway through the cooking time.
3. Turn the heat to 350 degrees F; continue to cook for about 15 minutes or until cooked through.
4. Let the duck breasts rest for 10 minutes before carving and serving. Bon appétit!

Chicken Tenders with Veggies

Prep Time: 10 minutes | Cook Time: 20 minutes | Serves 4

- 1 pound chicken tenders
- 1 tablespoon honey
- Pinch salt
- Freshly ground black pepper
- ½ cup soft fresh bread crumbs
- ½ teaspoon dried thyme
- 1 tablespoon olive oil
- 2 carrots, sliced
- 12 small red potatoes

1. In a medium bowl, toss the chicken tenders with the honey, salt, and pepper.
2. In a shallow bowl, combine the bread crumbs, thyme, and olive oil, and mix.
3. Coat the tenders in the bread crumbs, pressing firmly onto the meat.
4. Place the carrots and potatoes in the air fryer basket and top with the chicken tenders.
5. Roast for 18 to 20 minutes or until the chicken is cooked to 165°F and the vegetables are tender, shaking the basket halfway during the cooking time.

Curried Chicken with Fruit

Prep Time: 12 minutes | Cook Time: 18 minutes | Serves 4

- 3 (5-ounce) low-sodium boneless skinless chicken breasts, cut into 1½-inch cubes (see Tip)
- 2 teaspoons olive oil
- 2 tablespoons cornstarch
- 1 tablespoon curry powder
- 1 tart apple, chopped
- ½ cup low-sodium chicken broth
- ⅓ cup dried cranberries
- 2 tablespoons freshly squeezed orange juice
- Brown rice, cooked (optional)

1. In a medium bowl, mix the chicken and olive oil. Sprinkle with the cornstarch and curry powder. Toss to coat. Stir in the apple and transfer to a 6-by-2-inch metal pan. Bake in the air fryer for 8 minutes, stirring once during cooking.
2. Add the chicken broth, cranberries, and orange juice. Bake for about 10 minutes more, or until the sauce is slightly thickened and the chicken reaches an internal temperature of 165°F on a meat thermometer. Serve over hot cooked brown rice, if desired.

Italian Chicken Thighs

Prep Time: 10 minutes | Cook Time: 20 minutes | Serves 4

- 4 skin-on bone-in chicken thighs
- 2 tbsp. unsalted butter, melted
- 3 tsp. Italian herbs
- ½ tsp. garlic powder
- ¼ tsp. onion powder

1. Using a brush, coat the chicken thighs with the melted butter. Combine the herbs with the garlic powder and onion powder, then massage into the chicken thighs. Place the thighs in the fryer.
2. Cook at 380°F for 20 minutes, turning the chicken halfway through to cook on the other side.
3. When the thighs have achieved a golden color, test the temperature with a meat thermometer. Once they have reached 165°F, remove from the fryer and serve.

Teriyaki Chicken Wings

Prep Time: 15 minutes | Cook Time: 30 minutes | Serves 4

- ¼ tsp. ground ginger
- 2 tsp. minced garlic
- ½ cup sugar-free teriyaki sauce
- 2 lb. chicken wings
- 2 tsp. baking powder

1. In a small bowl, combine together the ginger, garlic, and teriyaki sauce. Place the chicken wings in a separate, larger bowl and pour the mixture over them. Toss to coat until the chicken is well covered.
2. Refrigerate for at least an hour.
3. Remove the marinated wings from the fridge and add the baking powder, tossing again to coat. Then place the chicken in the basket of your air fryer.
4. Cook for 25 minutes at 400°F, giving the basket a shake intermittently throughout the cooking time.
5. When the wings are 165°F and golden in color, remove from the fryer and serve immediately.

Chimichurri Turkey

Prep Time: 30 minutes | Cook Time: 40 minutes | Serves 1

- 1 lb. turkey breast
- ½ cup chimichurri sauce
- ½ cup butter
- ¼ cup parmesan cheese, grated
- ¼ tsp. garlic powder

1. Massage the chimichurri sauce into the turkey breast, then refrigerate in an airtight container for at least a half hour.
2. In the meantime, prepare the herbed butter. Mix together the butter, parmesan, and garlic powder, using a hand mixer if desired (this will make it extra creamy)
3. Preheat your fryer at 350°F and place a rack inside. Remove the turkey from the refrigerator and allow to return to room temperature for roughly twenty minutes while the fryer warms.
4. Place the turkey in the fryer and allow to cook for twenty minutes. Flip and cook on the other side for a further twenty minutes.
5. Take care when removing the turkey from the fryer. Place it on a serving dish and enjoy with the herbed butter.

Chicken Pizza Crusts

Prep Time: 10 minutes | Cook Time: 25 minutes | Serves 1

- ½ cup mozzarella, shredded
- ¼ cup parmesan cheese, grated
- 1 lb. ground chicken

1. In a large bowl, combine all the ingredients and then spread the mixture out, dividing it into four parts of equal size.
2. Cut a sheet of parchment paper into four circles, roughly six inches in diameter, and put some of the chicken mixture onto the center of each piece, flattening the mixture to fill out the circle.
3. Depending on the size of your fryer, cook either one or two circles at a time at 375°F for 25 minutes. Halfway through, turn the crust over to cook on the other side. Keep each batch warm while you move onto the next one.
4. Once all the crusts are cooked, top with cheese and the toppings of your choice. If desired, cook the topped crusts for an additional five minutes.
5. Serve hot, or freeze and save for later!

Crispy Chicken Thighs

Prep Time: 10 minutes | Cook Time: 25 minutes | Serves 1

- 1 lb. chicken thighs
- Salt and pepper
- 2 cups roasted pecans
- 1 cup water
- 1 cup flour

1. Preheat your fryer to 400°F.
2. Season the chicken with salt and pepper, then set aside.
3. Pulse the roasted pecans in a food processor until a flour-like consistency is achieved.
4. Fill a dish with the water, another with the flour, and a third with the pecans.
5. Coat the thighs with the flour. Mix the remaining flour with the processed pecans.
6. Dredge the thighs in the water and then press into the -pecan mix, ensuring the chicken is completely covered.
7. Cook the chicken in the fryer for twenty-two minutes, with an extra five minutes added if you would like the chicken a darker-brown color. Check the temperature has reached 165°F before serving.

Chicken Nuggets

Prep Time: 20 minutes | Cook Time: 280minutes | Serves 24 nuggets

- 1 pound boneless, skinless chicken thighs, cut into 1-inch chunks
- ¾ teaspoon salt
- ½ teaspoon black pepper
- ½ teaspoon garlic powder
- ½ teaspoon onion powder
- ½ cup flour
- 2 eggs, beaten
- ½ cup panko breadcrumbs
- 3 tablespoons plain breadcrumbs
- oil for misting or cooking spray

1. In the bowl of a food processor, combine chicken, ½ teaspoon salt, pepper, garlic powder, and onion powder. Process in short pulses until chicken is very finely chopped and well blended.
2. Place flour in one shallow dish and beaten eggs in another. In a third dish or plastic bag, mix together the panko crumbs, plain breadcrumbs, and ¼ teaspoon salt.
3. Shape chicken mixture into small nuggets. Dip nuggets in flour, then eggs, then panko crumb mixture.
4. Spray nuggets on both sides with oil or cooking spray and place in air fryer basket in a single layer, close but not overlapping.
5. Cook at 360°F for 10 minutes. Spray with oil and cook 3 to 4 minutes, until chicken is done and coating is golden brown.
6. Repeat step 5 to cook remaining nuggets.

Restaurant-Style Fried Chicken

Prep Time: 3 minutes | Cook Time: 12 minutes | Serves 4

- 1 pound chicken fillets
- 1 egg
- 1 tablespoon olive oil
- 1 cup crackers, crushed
- 1 tablespoon fresh coriander, minced
- 1 tablespoon fresh parsley, minced
- Sea salt and ground black pepper, to taste
- 1/4 teaspoon ground cumin
- 1/4 teaspoon mustard seeds
- 1 teaspoon celery seeds

1. Pat the chicken fillets dry with paper towels. Whisk the egg in a shallow bowl.
2. Mix the remaining ingredients in a separate shallow bowl.
3. Dip the chicken breasts into the egg mixture. Then, roll the chicken breasts over the breadcrumb mixture.
4. Cook the chicken at 380 degrees F for 12 minutes, turning them over halfway through the cooking time.
5. Bon appétit!

Chicken Hand Pies

Prep Time: 30 minutes | Cook Time: 20 minutes | Serves 8 pies

- ¾ cup chicken broth
- ¾ cup frozen mixed peas and carrots
- 1 cup cooked chicken, chopped
- 1 tablespoon cornstarch
- 1 tablespoon milk
- salt and pepper
- 1 8-count can organic flaky biscuits
- oil for misting or cooking spray

1. In a medium saucepan, bring chicken broth to a boil. Stir in the frozen peas and carrots and cook for 5 minutes over medium heat. Stir in chicken.
2. Mix the cornstarch into the milk until it dissolves. Stir it into the simmering chicken broth mixture and cook just until thickened.
3. Remove from heat, add salt and pepper to taste, and let cool slightly.
4. Lay biscuits out on wax paper. Peel each biscuit apart in the middle to make 2 rounds so you have 16 rounds total. Using your hands or a rolling pin, flatten each biscuit round slightly to make it larger and thinner.
5. Divide chicken filling among 8 of the biscuit rounds. Place remaining biscuit rounds on top and press edges all around. Use the tines of a fork to crimp biscuit edges and make sure they are sealed well.
6. Spray both sides lightly with oil or cooking spray.
7. Cook in a single layer, 4 at a time, at 330°F for 10 minutes or until biscuit dough is cooked through and golden brown.

Strawberry Turkey

Prep Time: 30 minutes | Cook Time: 20 minutes | Serves 2

- 2 lb. turkey breast
- 1 tbsp. olive oil
- Salt and pepper
- 1 cup fresh strawberries

1. Pre-heat your fryer to 375°F.
2. Massage the turkey breast with olive oil, before seasoning with a generous amount of salt and pepper.
3. Cook the turkey in the fryer for fifteen minutes. Flip the turkey and cook for a further fifteen minutes.
4. During these last fifteen minutes, blend the strawberries in a food processor until a smooth consistency has been achieved.
5. Heap the strawberries over the turkey, then cook for a final seven minutes and enjoy.

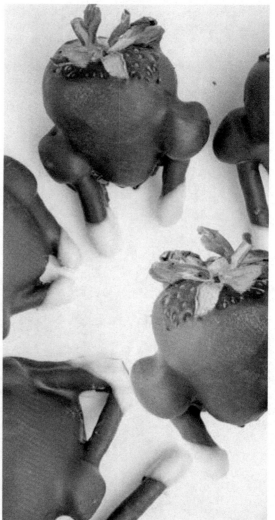

Betty's Baked Chicken

Prep Time: 10 minutes | Cook Time: 60 minutes | Serves 1

- ½ cup butter
- 1 tsp. pepper
- 3 tbsp. garlic, minced
- 1 whole chicken

1. Preheat your fryer at 350°F.
2. Allow the butter to soften at room temperature, then mix well in a small bowl with the pepper and garlic.
3. Massage the butter into the chicken. Any remaining butter can go inside the chicken.
4. Cook the chicken in the fryer for half an hour. Flip, then cook on the other side for another thirty minutes.
5. Test the temperature of the chicken by sticking a meat thermometer into the fat of the thigh to make sure it has reached 165°F. Take care when removing the chicken from the fryer. Let sit for ten minutes before you carve it and serve.

Creamy Chicken and Gnocchi

Prep Time: 10 minutes | Cook Time: 13 minutes | Serves 4

- 1 (1-pound) package shelf-stable gnocchi
- 1¼ cups low-sodium chicken stock
- ½ teaspoon kosher salt or ¼ teaspoon fine salt
- 1 pound chicken breast, cut into 1-inch chunks
- 1 cup heavy (whipping) cream
- 2 tablespoons sun-dried tomato purée
- 1 garlic clove, minced or smashed
- 1 cup frozen spinach, thawed and drained
- 1 cup grated Parmesan cheese

1. Place the gnocchi in an even layer on the sheet pan. Pour the chicken stock over the gnocchi.
2. Select BAKE, set temperature to 450°F, and set time to 7 minutes. Select START/PAUSE to begin preheating.
3. Once the unit has preheated, slide the pan into the oven.
4. While the gnocchi are cooking, sprinkle the salt over the chicken pieces. In a small bowl, mix together the cream, tomato purée, and garlic.
5. When cooking is complete, blot off any remaining stock, or drain the gnocchi and return it to the pan. Top the gnocchi with the spinach and chicken. Pour the cream mixture over the ingredients on the pan.
6. Select AIR ROAST, set temperature to 400°F, and set time to 6 minutes. Select START/PAUSE to begin preheating.
7. Once the unit has preheated, slide the pan into the oven.
8. After 4 minutes, remove the pan from the oven and gently stir the ingredients. Return the pan to the oven and continue cooking.
9. When cooking is complete, the gnocchi should be tender and the chicken should be cooked through. Remove the pan from the oven. Stir in the Parmesan cheese until it's melted, and serve.

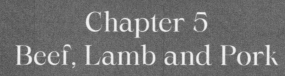

Chapter 5
Beef, Lamb and Pork

Steak Fajitas

Prep Time: 10 minutes | Cook Time: 15 minutes | Serves 4

- 8 (6-inch) flour or corn tortillas
- 1 pound top sirloin steak, sliced ¼-inch thick
- 1 red bell pepper, seeded and sliced ½-inch thick
- 1 green bell pepper, seeded and sliced ½-inch thick
- 1 jalapeño, seeded and sliced thin
- 1 medium onion, sliced ½-inch thick
- 2 tablespoons vegetable oil
- 2 tablespoons Mexican seasoning
- 1 teaspoon kosher salt or ½ teaspoon fine salt
- Salsa
- 1 small avocado, sliced

1. Place a large sheet of aluminum foil on the sheet pan. Place the tortillas on the foil in two stacks and wrap in the foil.
2. Select AIR ROAST, set temperature to 325°F, and set time to 6 minutes. Select START/PAUSE to begin preheating.
3. Once the unit has preheated, slide the pan into the oven. After 3 minutes, remove the pan from the oven and flip the packet of tortillas over. Return the pan to the oven and continue cooking.
4. While the tortillas warm, place the steak, bell peppers, jalapeño, and onion in a large bowl and drizzle the oil over. Sprinkle with the Mexican seasoning and salt, and toss to coat.
5. When cooking is complete, remove the pan from the oven and place the packet of tortillas on top of the oven to keep warm. Place the beef and peppers mixture on the sheet pan, spreading out into a single layer as much as possible.
6. Select AIR ROAST, set temperature to 375°F, and set time to 9 minutes. Select START/PAUSE to begin preheating.
7. Once the unit has preheated, slide the pan into the oven.
8. After about 5 minutes, remove the pan from the oven and stir the ingredients. Return the pan to the oven and continue cooking.
9. When cooking is complete, the vegetables will be soft and browned in places, and the beef will be browned on the outside and barely pink inside. Remove the pan from the oven. Unwrap the tortillas and spoon the fajita mixture into the tortillas. Serve with salsa and avocado slices

Beef and Crispy Broccoli

Prep Time: 10 minutes | Cook Time: 15 minutes | Serves 4

- 12 ounces broccoli florets (about 4 cups)
- 1 pound sirloin or flat iron steak, cut into thin strips
- ½ teaspoon kosher salt or ¼ teaspoon fine salt
- ¾ cup Asian-Style Sauce
- 1 teaspoon sriracha or chile-garlic sauce
- 3 tablespoons freshly squeezed orange juice
- 1 teaspoon cornstarch
- 1 medium onion, thinly sliced

1. Place a large piece of aluminum foil on the sheet pan. Place the broccoli on top and sprinkle with 3 tablespoons of water. Seal the broccoli in the foil in a single layer.
2. Select AIR ROAST, set temperature to 375°F, and set time to 6 minutes. Select START/PAUSE to begin preheating.
3. Once the unit has preheated, slide the pan into the oven.
4. While the broccoli steams, sprinkle the steak with the salt. In a small bowl, whisk together the Asian-Style Sauce, sriracha, orange juice, and cornstarch. Place the onion and beef in a large bowl.
5. When cooking is complete, remove the pan from the oven. Open the packet of broccoli and use tongs to transfer the broccoli to the bowl with the beef and onion, discarding the foil and remaining water. Pour the sauce over the beef and vegetables and toss to coat. Place the mixture on the sheet pan.
6. Select AIR ROAST, set temperature to 375°F, and set time to 9 minutes. Select START/PAUSE to begin preheating.
7. Once the unit has preheated, slide the pan into the oven.
8. After about 4 minutes, remove the pan from the oven and gently toss the ingredients. Return the pan to oven and continue cooking.
9. When cooking is complete, the sauce should be thickened, the vegetables tender, and the beef barely pink in the center. Serve plain or with steamed rice or Oven Rice.

Classic Pulled Beef

Prep Time: 10 minutes | Cook Time: 70 minutes | Serves 4

- 1 ½ pounds beef brisket
- 2 tablespoons olive oil
- 3 garlic cloves, pressed
- Sea salt and ground black pepper, to taste
- 1 teaspoon red pepper flakes, crushed
- 2 tablespoons tomato ketchup
- 2 tablespoons Dijon mustard

1. Toss the beef brisket with the olive oil, garlic, salt, black pepper, and red pepper; now, place the beef brisket in the Air Fryer cooking basket.
2. Cook the beef brisket at 390 degrees F for 15 minutes, turn the beef over and reduce the temperature to 360 degrees F.
3. Continue to cook the beef brisket for approximately 55 minutes or until cooked through.
4. Shred the beef with two forks; add in the ketchup and mustard and stir to combine well. Bon appétit!

Natchitoches Meat Pies

Prep Time: 20 minutes | Cook Time: 6 minutes per batch | Serves 4

- Filling
- ½ pound lean ground beef
- ¼ cup finely chopped onion
- ¼ cup finely chopped green bell pepper
- ⅛ teaspoon salt
- ½ teaspoon garlic powder
- ½ teaspoon red pepper flakes
- 1 tablespoon low sodium Worcestershire sauce
- Crust
- 2 cups self-rising flour
- ¼ cup butter, finely diced
- 1 cup milk
- Egg Wash
- 1 egg
- 1 tablespoon water or milk
- oil for misting or cooking spray

1. Mix all filling ingredients well and shape into 4 small patties.
2. Cook patties in air fryer basket at 390°F for 10 to 12 minutes or until well done.
3. Place patties in large bowl and use fork and knife to crumble meat into very small pieces. Set aside.
4. To make the crust, use a pastry blender or fork to cut the butter into the flour until well mixed. Add milk and stir until dough stiffens.
5. Divide dough into 8 equal portions.
6. On a lightly floured surface, roll each portion of dough into a circle. The circle should be thin and about 5 inches in diameter, but don't worry about getting a perfect shape. Uneven circles result in a rustic look that many people prefer.
7. Spoon 2 tablespoons of meat filling onto each dough circle.
8. Brush egg wash all the way around the edge of dough circle, about ½-inch deep. (See Tip.)
9. Fold each circle in half and press dough with tines of a dinner fork to seal the edges all the way around.
10. Brush tops of sealed meat pies with egg wash.
11. Cook filled pies in a single layer in air fryer basket at 360°F for 4 minutes. Spray tops with oil or cooking spray, turn pies over, and spray bottoms with oil or cooking spray. Cook for an additional 2 minutes.
12. Repeat previous step to cook remaining pies.

Pepperoni Pockets

Prep Time: 10 minutes | Cook Time: 10 minutes | Serves 4

- 4 bread slices, 1-inch thick
- olive oil for misting
- 24 slices pepperoni (about 2 ounces)
- 1 ounce roasted red peppers, drained and patted dry
- 1 ounce Pepper Jack cheese cut into 4 slices
- pizza sauce (optional)

1. Spray both sides of bread slices with olive oil.
2. Stand slices upright and cut a deep slit in the top to create a pocket—almost to the bottom crust but not all the way through.
3. Stuff each bread pocket with 6 slices of pepperoni, a large strip of roasted red pepper, and a slice of cheese.
4. Place bread pockets in air fryer basket, standing up. Cook at 360°F for 8 to 10 minutes, until filling is heated through and bread is lightly browned. Serve while hot as is or with pizza sauce for dipping

Brown Rice and Beef-Stuffed Bell Peppers

Prep Time: 10 minutes | Cook Time: 16 minutes | Serves 4

- 4 medium bell peppers, any colors, rinsed, tops removed
- 1 medium onion, chopped
- ½ cup grated carrot
- 2 teaspoons olive oil
- 2 medium beefsteak tomatoes, chopped
- 1 cup cooked brown rice
- 1 cup chopped cooked low-sodium roast beef (see Tip)
- 1 teaspoon dried marjoram

1. Remove the stems from the bell pepper tops and chop the tops.
2. In a 6-by-2-inch pan, combine the chopped bell pepper tops, onion, carrot, and olive oil. Cook for 2 to 4 minutes, or until the vegetables are crisp-tender.
3. Transfer the vegetables to a medium bowl. Add the tomatoes, brown rice, roast beef, and marjoram. Stir to mix.
4. Stuff the vegetable mixture into the bell peppers. Place the bell peppers in the air fryer basket. Bake for 11 to 16 minutes, or until the peppers are tender and the filling is hot. Serve immediately.

Pizza Tortilla Rolls

Prep Time: 15 minutes | Cook Time: 8 minutes per batch | Serves 4

- 1 teaspoon butter
- ½ medium onion, slivered
- ½ red or green bell pepper, julienned
- 4 ounces fresh white mushrooms, chopped
- 8 flour tortillas (6- or 7-inch size)
- ½ cup pizza sauce
- 8 thin slices deli ham
- 24 pepperoni slices (about 1½ ounces)
- 1 cup shredded mozzarella cheese (about 4 ounces)
- oil for misting or cooking spray

1. Place butter, onions, bell pepper, and mushrooms in air fryer baking pan. Cook at 390°F for 3 minutes. Stir and cook 3 to 4 minutes longer until just crisp and tender. Remove pan and set aside.
2. To assemble rolls, spread about 2 teaspoons of pizza sauce on one half of each tortilla. Top with a slice of ham and 3 slices of pepperoni. Divide sautéed vegetables among tortillas and top with cheese.
3. Roll up tortillas, secure with toothpicks if needed, and spray with oil.
4. Place 4 rolls in air fryer basket and cook for 4 minutes. Turn and cook 3 to 4 minutes, until heated through and lightly browned.
5. Repeat step 4 to cook remaining pizza rolls.

Pork & Beef Egg Rolls

Prep Time: 30 minutes | Cook Time: 8 minutes per batch | Serves 8

- ¼ pound very lean ground beef
- ¼ pound lean ground pork
- 1 tablespoon soy sauce
- 1 teaspoon olive oil
- ½ cup grated carrots
- 2 green onions, chopped
- 2 cups grated Napa cabbage
- ¼ cup chopped water chestnuts
- ¼ teaspoon salt
- ¼ teaspoon garlic powder
- ¼ teaspoon black pepper
- 1 egg
- 1 tablespoon water
- 8 egg roll wraps
- oil for misting or cooking spray

1. In a large skillet, brown beef and pork with soy sauce. Remove cooked meat from skillet, drain, and set aside.
2. Pour off any excess grease from skillet. Add olive oil, carrots, and onions. Sauté until barely tender, about 1 minute.
3. Stir in cabbage, cover, and cook for 1 minute or just until cabbage slightly wilts. Remove from heat.
4. In a large bowl, combine the cooked meats and vegetables, water chestnuts, salt, garlic powder, and pepper. Stir well. If needed, add more salt to taste.
5. Beat together egg and water in a small bowl.
6. Fill egg roll wrappers, using about ¼ cup of filling for each wrap. Roll up and brush all over with egg wash to seal. Spray very lightly with olive oil or cooking spray.
7. Place 4 egg rolls in air fryer basket and cook at 390°F for 4 minutes. Turn over and cook 3 to 4 more minutes, until golden brown and crispy.
8. Repeat to cook remaining egg rolls.

Dad's Spicy Burgers

Prep Time: 5 minutes | Cook Time: 15 minutes | Serves 3

- 3/4 pound ground beef
- 2 tablespoons onion, minced
- 1 teaspoon garlic, minced
- 1 teaspoon cayenne pepper
- Sea salt and ground black pepper, to taste
- 1 teaspoon red chili powder
- 3 hamburger buns

1. Mix the beef, onion, garlic, cayenne pepper, salt, black pepper, and red chili powder until everything is well combined. Form the mixture into three patties.
2. Cook the burgers at 380 degrees F for about 15 minutes or until cooked through; make sure to turn them over halfway through the cooking time.
3. Serve your burgers on the prepared buns and enjoy!

Marinated London Broil

Prep Time: 5 minutes | Cook Time: 28 minutes | Serves 4

- 1 pound London broil
- Kosher salt and ground black pepper, to taste
- 2 tablespoons olive oil
- 1 small lemon, freshly squeezed
- 3 cloves garlic, minced
- 1 tablespoon fresh parsley, chopped
- 1 tablespoon fresh coriander, chopped

1. Toss the beef with the remaining ingredients and let it marinate for an hour.
2. Place the beef in a lightly oiled Air Fryer cooking basket and discard the marinade.
3. Cook the beef at 400 degrees F for 28 minutes, turning it over halfway through the cooking time.
4. Bon appétit!

Greek Vegetable Skillet

Prep Time: 10 minutes | Cook Time: 19 minutes | Serves 4

- ½ pound 96 percent lean ground beef
- 2 medium tomatoes, chopped
- 1 onion, chopped
- 2 garlic cloves, minced
- 2 cups fresh baby spinach (see Tip)
- 2 tablespoons freshly squeezed lemon juice
- ⅓ cup low-sodium beef broth
- 2 tablespoons crumbled low-sodium feta cheese

1. In a 6-by-2-inch metal pan, crumble the beef. Cook in the air fryer for 3 to 7 minutes, stirring once during cooking, until browned. Drain off any fat or liquid.
2. Add the tomatoes, onion, and garlic to the pan. Air-fry for 4 to 8 minutes more, or until the onion is tender.
3. Add the spinach, lemon juice, and beef broth. Air-fry for 2 to 4 minutes more, or until the spinach is wilted.
4. Sprinkle with the feta cheese and serve immediately.

Beef Meatloaf

Prep Time: 5minutes | Cook Time: 25 minutes | Serves 4

- ¾ lb. ground chuck
- ¼ lb. ground pork sausage
- 1 cup shallots, finely chopped
- 2 eggs, well beaten
- 3 tbsp. plain milk
- 1 tbsp. oyster sauce
- 1 tsp. porcini mushrooms
- ½ tsp. cumin powder
- 1 tsp. garlic paste
- 1 tbsp. fresh parsley
- Seasoned salt and crushed red pepper flakes to taste
- 1 cup crushed saltines

1. Mix together all of the ingredients in a large bowl, combining everything well.
2. Transfer to the Air Fryer baking dish and cook at 360°F for 25 minutes.
3. Serve hot.

Light Herbed Meatballs

Prep Time: 10 minutes | Cook Time: 17 minutes | Serves 24 meatballs

- 1 medium onion, minced
- 2 garlic cloves, minced
- 1 teaspoon olive oil
- 1 slice low-sodium whole-wheat bread, crumbled
- 3 tablespoons 1 percent milk
- 1 teaspoon dried marjoram
- 1 teaspoon dried basil
- 1 pound 96 percent lean ground beef

1. In a 6-by-2-inch pan, combine the onion, garlic, and olive oil. Air-fry for 2 to 4 minutes, or until the vegetables are crisp-tender.
2. Transfer the vegetables to a medium bowl, and add the bread crumbs, milk, marjoram, and basil. Mix well.
3. Add the ground beef. With your hands, work the mixture gently but thoroughly until combined. Form the meat mixture into about 24 (1-inch) meatballs.
4. Bake the meatballs, in batches, in the air fryer basket for 12 to 17 minutes, or until they reach 160°F on a meat thermometer. Serve immediately.

Spicy Top Round Roast

Prep Time: 5 minutes | Cook Time: 55 minutes | Serves 5

- 2 pounds top round roast
- 2 tablespoons extra-virgin olive oil
- 2 cloves garlic, pressed
- 1 tablespoon fresh rosemary, chopped
- 1 tablespoon fresh parsley, chopped
- 1 teaspoon red chili powder
- Kosher salt and freshly ground black pepper, to taste

1. Toss the beef with the remaining ingredients; place the beef in the Air Fryer cooking basket.
2. Cook the beef at 390 degrees F for 55 minutes, turning it over halfway through the cooking time.
3. Enjoy!

Meatballs in Spicy Tomato Sauce

Prep Time: 10 minutes | Cook Time: 15 minutes | Serves 4

- 3 green onions, minced
- 1 garlic clove, minced
- 1 egg yolk
- ¼ cup saltine cracker crumbs
- Pinch salt
- Freshly ground black pepper
- 1 pound 95 percent lean ground beef
- Olive oil for misting
- 1¼ cups pasta sauce (from a 16-ounce jar)
- 2 tablespoons Dijon mustard

1. In a large bowl, combine the green onions, garlic, egg yolk, cracker crumbs, salt, and pepper, and mix well.
2. Add the ground beef and mix gently but thoroughly with your hands until combined. Form into 1½-inch meatballs.
3. Mist the meatballs with olive oil and put into the basket of the air fryer.
4. Bake for 8 to 11 minutes or until the meatballs are 165°F.
5. Remove the meatballs from the basket and place in a 6-inch metal bowl. Top with the pasta sauce and Dijon mustard and mix gently.
6. Bake for 3 to 4 minutes or until the sauce is hot.

Mexican Pizza

Prep Time: 10 minutes | Cook Time: 9 minutes | Serves 4

- ¾ cup refried beans (from a 16-ounce can)
- ½ cup salsa
- 10 frozen precooked beef meatballs, thawed and sliced
- 1 jalapeño pepper, sliced
- 4 whole-wheat pita breads
- 1 cup shredded pepper Jack cheese
- ½ cup shredded Colby cheese
- ⅓ cup sour cream

1. In a medium bowl, combine the refried beans, salsa, meatballs, and jalapeño pepper.
2. Preheat the air fryer for 3 to 4 minutes or until hot.
3. Top the pitas with the refried bean mixture and sprinkle with the cheeses.
4. Bake for 7 to 9 minutes or until the pizza is crisp and the cheese is melted and starts to brown.
5. Top each pizza with a dollop of sour cream and serve warm.

Tex-Mex Steak

Prep Time: 25 minutes | Cook Time: 20 minutes | Serves 4

- 1 pound skirt steak
- 1 chipotle pepper in adobo sauce, minced (La Costena or another gluten-free brand)
- 2 tablespoons adobo sauce (La Costena or another gluten-free brand)
- ½ teaspoon salt
- ⅛ teaspoon pepper
- ⅛ teaspoon crushed red pepper flakes

1. Cut the steak into four pieces and place them on a plate.
2. In a small bowl, combine the minced chipotle pepper, adobo sauce, salt, pepper, and crushed red pepper flakes. Spread over the steaks on both sides.
3. Let the steaks stand at room temperature for at least 20 minutes, or refrigerate up to 12 hours.
4. Grill the steaks, two at a time, in the air fryer basket for 10 minutes until the steaks register an internal temperature of at least 145°F. Repeat with remaining steaks while the first ones rest, covered with foil.
5. Add the just-cooked steaks to the ones that have been resting and let rest for another 5 minutes. Slice thinly across the grain to serve.

Asian Beef Burgers

Prep Time: 8 minutes | Cook Time: 15 minutes | Serves 4

- ¾ lb. lean ground beef
- 1 tbsp. soy sauce
- 1 tsp. Dijon mustard
- Few dashes of liquid smoke
- 1 tsp. shallot powder
- 1 clove garlic, minced
- ½ tsp. cumin powder
- ¼ cup scallions, minced
- ⅓ tsp. sea salt flakes
- ⅓ tsp. freshly cracked mixed peppercorns
- 1 tsp. celery seeds
- 1 tsp. parsley flakes

1. Mix together all of the ingredients in a bowl using your hands, combining everything well.
2. Take four equal amounts of the mixture and mold each one into a patty.
3. Use the back of a spoon to create a shallow dip in the center of each patty. This will prevent them from puffing up during the cooking process.
4. Lightly coat all sides of the patties with cooking spray.
5. Place each one in the Air Fryer and cook for roughly 12 minutes at 360°F.

Stuffed Bell Pepper

Prep Time: 10 minutes | Cook Time: 15 minutes | Serves 4

- 4 bell peppers, cut top of bell pepper
- 16 oz. ground beef
- 2/3 cup cheese, shredded
- ½ cup rice, cooked
- 1 tsp. basil, dried
- ½ tsp. chili powder
- 1 tsp. black pepper
- 1 tsp. garlic salt
- 2 tsp. Worcestershire sauce
- 8 oz. tomato sauce
- 2 garlic cloves, minced
- 1 small onion, chopped

1. Grease a frying pan with cooking spray and fry the onion and garlic over a medium heat.
2. Stir in the beef, basil, chili powder, black pepper, and garlic salt, combining everything well. Allow to cook until the beef is nicely browned, before taking the pan off the heat.
3. Add in half of the cheese, the rice, Worcestershire sauce, and tomato sauce and stir to combine.
4. Spoon equal amounts of the beef mixture into the four bell peppers, filling them entirely.
5. Pre-heat the Air Fryer at 400°F.
6. Spritz the Air Fryer basket with cooking spray.
7. Put the stuffed bell peppers in the basket and allow to cook for 11 minutes.
8. Add the remaining cheese on top of each bell pepper with remaining cheese and cook for a further 2 minutes. When the cheese is melted and the bell peppers are piping hot, serve immediately.

Chapter 6
Fish and Seafood

Shrimp with Celery and Toasted Cashews

Prep Time: 10 minutes | Cook Time: 10 minutes | Serves 4

- 1 cup roasted, salted cashews
- ½ cup Asian-Style Sauce
- 1 tablespoon sesame oil
- ½ teaspoon red pepper flakes
- 1 teaspoon cornstarch
- 1 tablespoon dry sherry (optional)
- 1¼ pound medium shrimp (21–25 or 25–30 count), peeled and deveined
- 6 scallions, thinly sliced, white and green parts separated
- 8 stalks celery, sliced on the diagonal about ⅓-inch thick

1. Place the cashews in the Air Fry basket.
2. Select AIR FRY, set temperature to 400°F, and set time to 25 minutes. Select START/PAUSE to begin preheating.
3. Once the unit has preheated, slide the basket into the oven. After 1 minute, check the cashews; if they are dark golden brown, remove the basket from the oven. If not, continue cooking for another 30 seconds to 1 minute. Set aside to cool.
4. In a small bowl, mix together the Asian-Style Sauce, sesame oil, red pepper flakes, cornstarch, and sherry (if using).
5. Place the shrimp in a medium bowl. Pour about one-third over the shrimp and toss to coat. Set aside.
6. Place the white parts of the scallions and celery on the sheet pan. Pour the remaining sauce over and toss to coat well.
7. Select AIR ROAST, set temperature to 375°F, and set time to 8 minutes. Select START/PAUSE to begin preheating.
8. Once the unit has preheated, slide the pan into the oven.
9. After 3 minutes, remove the pan from the oven. Add the shrimp and half of the green parts of the scallions to the celery mixture and stir to combine. Return the pan to the oven and finish cooking.
10. When cooking is complete, the shrimp should be pink and opaque. Remove the pan from the oven. Stir in the cashews and garnish with the remaining scallion greens. Serve with steamed rice, if desired.

Restaurant-Style Fried Calamari

Prep Time: 5 minutes | Cook Time: 5 minutes | Serves 4

- 1 cup all-purpose flour
- 1/2 cup tortilla chips, crushed
- 1 teaspoon mustard powder
- 1 tablespoon dried parsley
- Sea salt and freshly ground black pepper, to taste
- 1 teaspoon cayenne pepper
- 2 tablespoons olive oil
- 1 pound calamari, sliced into rings

1. In a mixing bowl, thoroughly combine the flour, tortilla chips, spices, and olive oil. Mix to combine well.
2. Now, dip your calamari into the flour mixture to coat.
3. Cook your calamari at 400 degrees F for 5 minutes, turning them over halfway through the cooking time.
4. Bon appétit!

Mom's Famous Fish Sticks

Prep Time: 5 minutes | Cook Time: 10 minutes | Serves 4

- 1/2 cup all-purpose flour
- 1 large egg
- 2 tablespoons buttermilk
- 1/2 cup crackers, crushed
- 1 teaspoon garlic powder
- Sea salt and ground black pepper, to taste
- 1/2 teaspoon cayenne pepper
- 1 pound tilapia fillets, cut into strips

1. In a shallow bowl, place the flour. Whisk the egg and buttermilk in a second bowl, and mix the crushed crackers and spices in a third bowl.
2. Dip the fish strips in the flour mixture, then in the whisked eggs; finally, roll the fish strips over the cracker mixture until they are well coated on all sides.
3. Arrange the fish sticks in the Air Fryer basket.
4. Cook the fish sticks at 400 degrees F for about 10 minutes, shaking the basket halfway through the cooking time.
5. Bon appétit!

Cheesy Lemon Halibut

Prep Time: 5 minutes | Cook Time: 15 minutes | Serves 2

- 1 lb. halibut fillet
- ½ cup butter
- 2 ½ tbsp. mayonnaise
- 2 ½ tbsp. lemon juice
- ¾ cup parmesan cheese, grated

1. Preheat your fryer at 375°F.
2. Spritz the halibut fillets with cooking spray and season as desired.
3. Put the halibut in the fryer and cook for twelve minutes.
4. In the meantime, combine the butter, mayonnaise, and lemon juice in a bowl with a hand mixer. Ensure a creamy texture is achieved.
5. Stir in the grated parmesan.
6. When the halibut is ready, open the drawer and spread the butter over the fish with a butter knife. Allow to cook for a further two minutes, then serve hot.

Fish Tacos with Jalapeño-Lime Sauce

Prep Time: 25 minutes | Cook Time: 10 minutes | Serves 4

- 1 pound fish fillets
- ¼ teaspoon cumin
- ¼ teaspoon coriander
- ⅛ teaspoon ground red pepper
- 1 tablespoon lime zest
- ¼ teaspoon smoked paprika
- 1 teaspoon oil
- cooking spray
- 6–8 corn or flour tortillas (6-inch size)
- ½ cup sour cream
- 1 tablespoon lime juice
- ¼ teaspoon grated lime zest
- ½ teaspoon minced jalapeño (flesh only)
- ¼ teaspoon cumin
- 1 cup shredded Napa cabbage
- ¼ cup slivered red or green bell pepper
- ¼ cup slivered onion

1. Slice the fish fillets into strips approximately ½-inch thick.
2. Put the strips into a sealable plastic bag along with the cumin, coriander, red pepper, lime zest, smoked paprika, and oil. Massage seasonings into the fish until evenly distributed.
3. Spray air fryer basket with nonstick cooking spray and place seasoned fish inside.
4. Cook at 390°F for approximately 5 minutes. Shake basket to distribute fish. Cook an additional 2 to 5 minutes, until fish flakes easily.
5. While the fish is cooking, prepare the Jalapeño-Lime Sauce by mixing the sour cream, lime juice, lime zest, jalapeño, and cumin together to make a smooth sauce. Set aside.
6. Mix the cabbage, bell pepper, and onion together and set aside.
7. To warm refrigerated tortillas, wrap in damp paper towels and microwave for 30 to 60 seconds.
8. To serve, spoon some of fish into a warm tortilla. Add one or two tablespoons Napa Cabbage Garnish and drizzle with Jalapeño-Lime Sauce.

Classic Garlic Shrimp

Prep Time: 4 minutes | Cook Time: 6 minutes | Serves 4

- 1 ½ pounds raw shrimp, peeled and deveined
- 1 tablespoon olive oil
- 1 teaspoon garlic, minced
- 1 teaspoon cayenne pepper
- 1/2 teaspoon lemon pepper
- Sea salt, to taste

1. Toss all ingredients in a lightly greased Air Fryer cooking basket.
2. Cook the shrimp at 400 degrees F for 6 minutes, tossing the basket halfway through the cooking time.
3. Bon appétit!

Flounder Fillets

Prep Time: 10 minutes | Cook Time: 8 minutes | Serves 4

- 1 egg white
- 1 tablespoon water
- 1 cup panko breadcrumbs
- 2 tablespoons extra-light virgin olive oil
- 4 4-ounce flounder fillets
- salt and pepper
- oil for misting or cooking spray

1. Preheat air fryer to 390°F.
2. Beat together egg white and water in shallow dish.
3. In another shallow dish, mix panko crumbs and oil until well combined and crumbly (best done by hand).
4. Season flounder fillets with salt and pepper to taste. Dip each fillet into egg mixture and then roll in panko crumbs, pressing in crumbs so that fish is nicely coated.
5. Spray air fryer basket with nonstick cooking spray and add fillets. Cook at 390°F for 3 minutes.
6. Spray fish fillets but do not turn. Cook 2 to 5 minutes longer or until golden brown and crispy. Using a spatula, carefully remove fish from basket and serve.

Italian Tuna Roast

Prep Time: 15 minutes | Cook Time: 24 minutes | Serves 8

- cooking spray
- 1 tablespoon Italian seasoning
- ⅛ teaspoon ground black pepper
- 1 tablespoon extra-light olive oil
- 1 teaspoon lemon juice
- 1 tuna loin (approximately 2 pounds, 3 to 4 inches thick, large enough to fill a 6 x 6-inch baking dish)

1. Spray baking dish with cooking spray and place in air fryer basket. Preheat air fryer to 390°F.
2. Mix together the Italian seasoning, pepper, oil, and lemon juice.
3. Using a dull table knife or butter knife, pierce top of tuna about every half inch. Insert knife into top of tuna roast and pierce almost all the way to the bottom.
4. Spoon oil mixture into each of the holes and use the knife to push seasonings into the tuna as deeply as possible.
5. Spread any remaining oil mixture on all outer surfaces of tuna.
6. Place tuna roast in baking dish and cook at 390°F for 20 minutes. Check temperature with a meat thermometer. Cook for an additional 1 to 4 minutes or until temperature reaches 145°F.
7. Remove basket from fryer and let tuna sit in basket for 10 minutes.

Teriyaki Salmon with Baby Bok Choy

Prep Time: 15 minutes | Cook Time: 15 minutes | Serves 4

- ¾ cup Teriyaki Sauce or store-bought variety
- 4 (6-ounce) skinless salmon fillets
- 4 heads baby bok choy, root ends trimmed off and cut in half lengthwise through the root
- 1 tablespoon vegetable oil
- 1 teaspoon sesame oil
- 1 tablespoon toasted sesame seeds

1. Set aside ¼ cup of Teriyaki Sauce and pour the rest into a resealable plastic bag. Place the salmon in the bag and seal, squeezing as much air out as possible. Let the salmon marinate for at least 10 minutes (longer if you have the time).
2. Place the bok choy halves on the sheet pan. Drizzle the vegetable and sesame oils over the vegetables and toss to coat. Drizzle about a tablespoon of the reserved Teriyaki Sauce over the bok choy, then push them to the sides of the pan.
3. Place the salmon fillets in the middle of the sheet pan.
4. Select AIR ROAST, set temperature to 375°F, and set time to 15 minutes. Select START/PAUSE to begin preheating.
5. Once the unit has preheated, slide the pan into the oven.
6. When cooking is complete, remove the pan from the oven. Brush the salmon with the remaining Teriyaki Sauce. Garnish with the sesame seeds. Serve with steamed rice, if desired.

Tuna Wraps

Prep Time: 10 minutes | Cook Time: 7 minutes | Serves 4

- 1 pound fresh tuna steak, cut into 1-inch cubes
- 1 tablespoon grated fresh ginger
- 2 garlic cloves, minced
- ½ teaspoon toasted sesame oil
- 4 low-sodium whole-wheat tortillas
- ¼ cup low-fat mayonnaise
- 2 cups shredded romaine lettuce (see Tip)
- 1 red bell pepper, thinly sliced

1. In a medium bowl, mix the tuna, ginger, garlic, and sesame oil. Let it stand for 10 minutes.
2. Grill the tuna in the air fryer for 4 to 7 minutes, or until done to your liking and lightly browned.
3. Make wraps with the tuna, tortillas, mayonnaise, lettuce, and bell pepper. Serve immediately.

Tuna and Fruit Kebabs

Prep Time: 15 minutes | Cook Time: 12 minutes | Serves 4

- 1 pound tuna steaks, cut into 1-inch cubes
- ½ cup canned pineapple chunks, drained, juice reserved
- ½ cup large red grapes
- 1 tablespoon honey
- 2 teaspoons grated fresh ginger
- 1 teaspoon olive oil
- Pinch cayenne pepper

1. Thread the tuna, pineapple, and grapes on 8 bamboo (see Tip) or 4 metal skewers that fit in the air fryer.
2. In a small bowl, whisk the honey, 1 tablespoon of reserved pineapple juice, the ginger, olive oil, and cayenne. Brush this mixture over the kebabs. Let them stand for 10 minutes.
3. Grill the kebabs for 8 to 12 minutes, or until the tuna reaches an internal temperature of at least 145°F on a meat thermometer, and the fruit is tender and glazed, brushing once with the remaining sauce. Discard any remaining marinade. Serve immediately.

Exotic Fried Prawns

Prep Time: 3 minutes | Cook Time: 9 minutes | Serves 4

- 1 ½ pounds prawns, peeled and deveined
- 2 garlic cloves, minced
- 2 tablespoons fresh chives, chopped
- 1/2 cup whole-wheat flour
- 1/2 teaspoon sweet paprika
- 1 teaspoon hot paprika
- Salt and freshly ground black pepper, to taste
- 2 tablespoons coconut oil
- 2 tablespoons lemon juice

1. Toss all ingredients in a lightly greased Air Fryer cooking basket.
2. Cook the prawns at 400 degrees F for 9 minutes, tossing the basket halfway through the cooking time.
3. Bon appétit!

Crispy Herbed Salmon

Prep Time: 5 minutes | Cook Time: 12 minutes | Serves 4

- 4 (6-ounce) skinless salmon fillets
- 3 tablespoons honey mustard
- ½ teaspoon dried thyme
- ½ teaspoon dried basil
- ¼ cup panko bread crumbs
- ⅓ cup crushed potato chips
- 2 tablespoons olive oil

1. Place the salmon on a plate. In a small bowl, combine the mustard, thyme, and basil, and spread evenly over the salmon.
2. In another small bowl, combine the bread crumbs and potato chips and mix well. Drizzle in the olive oil and mix until combined.
3. Place the salmon in the air fryer basket and gently but firmly press the bread crumb mixture onto the top of each fillet.
4. Bake for 9 to 12 minutes or until the salmon reaches at least 145°F on a meat thermometer and the topping is browned and crisp.

Spicy Mackerel

Prep Time: 8 minutes | Cook Time: 12 minutes | Serves 2

- 2 mackerel fillets
- 2 tbsp. red chili flakes
- 2 tsp. garlic, minced
- 1 tsp. lemon juice

1. Season the mackerel fillets with the red pepper flakes, minced garlic, and a drizzle of lemon juice. Allow to sit for five minutes.
2. Preheat your fryer at 350°F.
3. Cook the mackerel for five minutes, before opening the drawer, flipping the fillets, and allowing to cook on the other side for another five minutes.
4. Plate the fillets, making sure to spoon any remaining juice over them before serving.

Cabbage Steaks

Prep Time: 2 minutes | Cook Time: 3 minutes | Serves 2

- small head cabbage
- 1 tsp. butter, butter
- 1 tsp. paprika
- 1 tsp. olive oil

1. Halve the cabbage.
2. In a bowl, mix together the melted butter, paprika, and olive oil. Massage into the cabbage slices, making sure to coat it well. Season as desired with salt and pepper or any other seasonings of your choosing.
3. Pre-heat the fryer at 400°F and set the rack inside.
4. Put the cabbage in the fryer and cook for three minutes. Flip it and cook on the other side for another two minutes. Enjoy!

Crispy Parmesan French Fries

Prep Time: 5 minutes | Cook Time: 10 minutes | Serves 4

- 4 cups frozen thin French fries
- 2 teaspoons olive oil
- ⅓ cup grated Parmesan cheese
- ½ teaspoon dried thyme
- ½ teaspoon dried basil
- ½ teaspoon salt

1. If there is any ice on the French fries, remove it. Place the French fries in the air fryer basket and drizzle with the olive oil. Toss gently.
2. Air-fry for about 10 minutes, or until the fries are golden brown and hot, shaking the basket once during cooking time.
3. Immediately put the fries into a serving bowl and sprinkle with the Parmesan, thyme, basil, and salt. Shake to coat and serve hot.

Cheesy Potato Pot

Prep Time: 10 minutes | Cook Time: 15 minutes | Serves 4

- 3 cups cubed red potatoes (unpeeled, cut into ½-inch cubes)
- ½ teaspoon garlic powder
- salt and pepper
- 1 tablespoon oil
- chopped chives for garnish (optional)
- 2 tablespoons milk
- 1 tablespoon butter
- 2 ounces sharp Cheddar cheese, grated
- 1 tablespoon sour cream

1. Place potato cubes in large bowl and sprinkle with garlic, salt, and pepper. Add oil and stir to coat well.
2. Cook at 390°F for 13 to 15 minutes or until potatoes are tender. Stir every 4 or 5 minutes during cooking time.

3. While potatoes are cooking, combine milk and butter in a small saucepan. Warm over medium-low heat to melt butter. Add cheese and stir until it melts. The melted cheese will remain separated from the milk mixture. Remove from heat until potatoes are done.
4. When ready to serve, add sour cream to cheese mixture and stir over medium-low heat just until warmed. Place cooked potatoes in serving bowl. Pour sauce over potatoes and stir to combine.
5. Garnish with chives if desired.

Scalloped Mixed Vegetables

Prep Time: 10 minutes | Cook Time: 20 minutes | Serves 4

- 1 Yukon Gold potato, thinly sliced
- 1 small sweet potato, peeled and thinly sliced
- 1 medium carrot, thinly sliced
- ¼ cup minced onion
- 3 garlic cloves, minced
- ¾ cup 2 percent milk
- 2 tablespoons cornstarch
- ½ teaspoon dried thyme

1. In a 6-by-2-inch pan, layer the potato, sweet potato, carrot, onion, and garlic.
2. In a small bowl, whisk the milk, cornstarch, and thyme until blended. Pour the milk mixture evenly over the vegetables in the pan.
3. Bake for 15 minutes. Check the casserole—it should be golden brown on top, and the vegetables should be tender. If they aren't, bake for 4 to 5 minutes more. Serve immediately.

Zucchini Gratin

Prep Time: 2 minutes | Cook Time: 13 minutes | Serves 4

- 5 oz. parmesan cheese, shredded
- 1 tbsp. coconut flour
- 1 tbsp. dried parsley
- 2 zucchinis
- 1 tsp. butter, melted

1. Mix the parmesan and coconut flour together in a bowl, seasoning with parsley to taste.
2. Cut the zucchini in half lengthwise and chop the halves into four slices.
3. Pre-heat the fryer at 400°F.
4. Pour the melted butter over the zucchini and then dip the zucchini into the parmesan-flour mixture, coating it all over. Cook the zucchini in the fryer for thirteen minutes.

Crispy Sweet Potato Wedges

Prep Time: 5 minutes | Cook Time: 25 minutes | Serves 4

- 2 sweet potatoes, peeled and cut into ½-inch wedges
- 2 teaspoons olive oil
- 2 tablespoons cornstarch
- 1 teaspoon ground cinnamon
- ¼ teaspoon ground allspice
- ¼ teaspoon ground nutmeg
- ⅛ teaspoon cayenne pepper

1. In a medium bowl of warm water, soak the sweet potato wedges for 10 minutes. Drain and pat dry with paper towels. Toss with the olive oil.
2. Put half the potato wedges into the air fryer basket and roast for 8 minutes. Transfer the fries to a large bowl (see Tip). Repeat with the remaining sweet potato wedges.
3. In the large bowl, sprinkle all the potatoes with the cornstarch and toss very thoroughly to coat; this should take at least 2 minutes.
4. Sprinkle with the cinnamon, allspice, nutmeg, and cayenne. Toss again.
5. Return half the wedges to the air fryer and roast for 12 to 17 minutes more, until the potatoes are golden brown and crisp, tossing the wedges in the basket twice during cooking.
6. Repeat with the remaining wedges. Serve immediately.

Creamed Cauliflower Salad with Bacon

Prep Time: 3 minutes | Cook Time: 12 minutes | Serves 3

- 3/4 pound cauliflower florets
- 2 ounces bacon, diced
- 1/4 cup sour cream
- 1/4 cup mayonnaise
- 1 teaspoon Dijon mustard
- 1 tablespoon apple cider vinegar
- 1 garlic clove, minced
- 1 small red onion, thinly sliced
- Kosher salt and freshly ground black pepper, to taste

1. Place the cauliflower florets in a lightly greased Air Fryer basket.
2. Cook the cauliflower florets at 400 degrees F for 12 minutes, shaking the basket halfway through the cooking time.
3. Thoroughly combine the cauliflower florets with the remaining ingredients. Serve well-chilled and enjoy!

Corn Croquettes

Prep Time: 10 minutes | Cook Time: 14 minutes | Serves 4

- ½ cup leftover mashed potatoes
- 2 cups corn kernels (if frozen, thawed, and well drained)
- ¼ teaspoon onion powder
- ⅛ teaspoon ground black pepper
- ¼ teaspoon salt
- ½ cup panko breadcrumbs
- oil for misting or cooking spray

1. Place the potatoes and half the corn in food processor and pulse until corn is well chopped.
2. Transfer mixture to large bowl and stir in remaining corn, onion powder, pepper and salt.
3. Shape mixture into 16 balls.
4. Roll balls in panko crumbs, mist with oil or cooking spray, and place in air fryer basket.
5. Cook at 360°F for 12 to 14 minutes, until golden brown and crispy.

Corn on the Cob

Prep Time: 5 minutes | Cook Time: 15 minutes | Serves 4

- 2 large ears fresh corn
- olive oil for misting
- salt (optional)

1. Shuck corn, remove silks, and wash.
2. Cut or break each ear in half crosswise.
3. Spray corn with olive oil.
4. Cook at 390°F for 12 to 15 minutes or until browned as much as you like.
5. Serve plain or with coarsely ground salt.

Scalloped Potatoes

Prep Time: 5 minutes | Cook Time: 20 minutes | Serves 4

- 2 cups pre-sliced refrigerated potatoes
- 3 cloves garlic, minced
- Pinch salt
- Freshly ground black pepper
- ¾ cup heavy cream

1. Layer the potatoes, garlic, salt, and pepper in a 6-by-6-by-2-inch baking pan. Slowly pour the cream over all.
2. Bake for 15 minutes, until the potatoes are golden brown on top and tender. Check their state and, if needed, bake for 5 minutes until browned.

Classic Broccoli Florets

Prep Time: 2 minutes | Cook Time: 6 minutes | Serves 3

- 3/4 pound broccoli florets
- 1 tablespoon olive oil
- 1 teaspoon garlic powder
- Sea salt and ground black pepper, to taste

1. Toss the broccoli florets with the remaining ingredients until well coated.
2. Arrange the broccoli florets in the Air Fryer basket.
3. Cook the broccoli florets at 395 degrees F for 6 minutes, shaking the basket halfway through the cooking time.
4. Bon appétit!

Tart & Spicy Indian Potatoes

Prep Time: 15 minutes | Cook Time: 45 minutes | Serves 4

- 4 cups quartered baby yellow potatoes
- 3 tablespoons vegetable oil
- 1 teaspoon ground turmeric
- 1 teaspoon amchoor (see headnote)
- 1 teaspoon kosher salt
- ¼ teaspoon ground cumin
- ¼ teaspoon ground coriander
- ¼ to ½ teaspoon cayenne pepper
- 1 tablespoon fresh lime or lemon juice
- ¼ cup chopped fresh cilantro or parsley

1. In a large bowl, toss together the potatoes, vegetable oil, turmeric, amchoor, salt, cumin, coriander, and cayenne until the potatoes are well coated.
2. Place the seasoned potatoes in the air-fryer basket. Set the air fryer to 400°F for 15 minutes, or until they are cooked through and tender when pierced with a fork.
3. Transfer the potatoes to a serving platter or bowl. Drizzle with the lime juice and sprinkle with the cilantro before serving.

Southern-Style Peaches
Prep Time: 5 minutes | Cook Time: 15 minutes | Serves 3

- 3 peaches, halved
- 1 tablespoon fresh lime juice
- 1/2 teaspoon ground cinnamon
- 1/2 teaspoon grated nutmeg
- 1/2 cup brown sugar
- 4 tablespoons coconut oil

1. Toss the peaches with the remaining ingredients.
2. Pour 1/4 cup of water into an Air Fryer safe dish. Place the peaches in the dish.
3. Bake the peaches at 340 degrees F for 15 minutes. Serve at room temperature. Bon appétit!

Fluffy Scones with Cranberries
Prep Time: 3 minutes | Cook Time: 17 minutes | Serves 4

- 1 cup all-purpose flour
- 1 teaspoon baking powder
- 1/4 cup caster sugar
- A pinch of sea salt
- 1/4 teaspoon ground cinnamon
- 4 tablespoons butter
- 1 egg, beaten
- 1/4 cup milk
- 2 ounces dried cranberries

1. Start by preheating your Air Fryer to 360 degrees F.
2. Mix all the ingredients until everything is well incorporated. Spoon the batter into baking cups; lower the cups into the Air Fryer basket.
3. Bake your scones for about 17 minutes or until a tester comes out dry and clean.
4. Bon appétit!

Coconut Rice Cake
Prep Time: 8 minutes | Cook Time: 35 minutes | Serves 8

- 1 cup all-natural coconut water
- 1 cup unsweetened coconut milk
- 1 teaspoon almond extract
- 1/4 teaspoon salt
- 4 tablespoons honey
- cooking spray
- 3/4 cup raw jasmine rice
- 2 cups sliced or cubed fruit

1. In a medium bowl, mix together the coconut water, coconut milk, almond extract, salt, and honey.
2. Spray air fryer baking pan with cooking spray and add the rice.
3. Pour liquid mixture over rice.
4. Cook at 360°F for 15 minutes. Stir and cook for 15 to 20 minutes longer or until rice grains are tender.
5. Allow cake to cool slightly. Run a dull knife around edge of cake, inside the pan. Turn the cake out onto a platter and garnish with fruit.

Custard
Prep Time: 8 minutes | Cook Time: 60 minutes | Serves 6

- 2 cups whole milk
- 2 eggs
- 1/4 cup sugar
- 1/8 teaspoon salt
- 1/4 teaspoon vanilla
- cooking spray
- 1/8 teaspoon nutmeg

1. In a blender, process milk, egg, sugar, salt, and vanilla until smooth.
2. Spray a 6 x 6-inch baking pan with nonstick spray and pour the custard into it.
3. Cook at 300°F for 45 to 60 minutes. Custard is done when the center sets.
4. Sprinkle top with the nutmeg.
5. Allow custard to cool slightly.
6. Serve it warm, at room temperature, or chilled.

Chocolate Peanut Butter Bread Pudding
Prep Time: 10 minutes | Cook Time: 12 minutes | Serves 8

- Nonstick baking spray with flour
- 1 egg
- 1 egg yolk
- 3/4 cup chocolate milk
- 2 tablespoons cocoa powder
- 3 tablespoons brown sugar
- 3 tablespoons peanut butter
- 1 teaspoon vanilla
- 5 slices firm white bread, cubed

1. Spray a 6-by-6-by-2-inch baking pan with nonstick spray.
2. In a medium bowl, combine the egg, egg yolk, chocolate milk, cocoa, brown sugar, peanut butter, and vanilla, and mix until combined. Stir in the bread cubes and let soak for 10 minutes.
3. Spoon this mixture into the prepared pan. Bake for 10 to 12 minutes or until the pudding is firm to the touch.

Coconut Pillow
Prep Time: 1-2 days | Cook Time: 0 minutes | Serves 4

- 1 can unsweetened coconut milk
- Berries of choice
- Dark chocolate

1. Refrigerate the coconut milk for 24 hours.
2. Remove it from your refrigerator and whip for 2-3 minutes.
3. Fold in the berries.
4. Season with the chocolate shavings.
5. Serve!

Strawberry-Rhubarb Crumble

Prep Time: 10 minutes | Cook Time: 17 minutes | Serves 6

- 1½ cups sliced fresh strawberries
- ¾ cup sliced rhubarb
- ⅓ cup sugar
- ⅔ cup quick-cooking oatmeal
- ½ cup whole-wheat pastry flour
- ¼ cup packed brown sugar
- ½ teaspoon ground cinnamon
- 3 tablespoons unsalted butter, melted

1. In a 6-by-2-inch metal pan, combine the strawberries, rhubarb, and sugar.
2. In a medium bowl, mix the oatmeal, pastry flour, brown sugar, and cinnamon.
3. Stir the melted butter into the oatmeal mixture until crumbly. Sprinkle this over the fruit. Bake for 12 to 17 minutes, or until the fruit is bubbling and the topping is golden brown. Serve warm.

Coffee Surprise

Prep Time: 5 minutes | Cook Time: 0 minutes | Serves 1

- 2 heaped tbsp flaxseed, ground
- 100ml cooking cream 35% fat
- ½ tsp cocoa powder, dark and unsweetened
- 1 tbsp goji berries
- Freshly brewed coffee

1. Mix together the flaxseeds, cream and cocoa and coffee.
2. Season with goji berries.
3. Serve!

Cinnamon Apple Wedges

Prep Time: 3 minutes | Cook Time: 17 minutes | Serves 2

- 2 apples, peeled, cored, and cut into wedges
- 2 teaspoons coconut oil
- 2 tablespoons brown sugar
- 1 teaspoon pure vanilla extract
- 1 teaspoon ground cinnamon
- 1/4 cup water

1. Toss the apples with the coconut oil, sugar, vanilla, and cinnamon.
2. Pour 1/4 cup of water into an Air Fryer safe dish. Place the apples in the dish.
3. Bake the apples at 340 degrees F for 17 minutes. Serve at room temperature. Bon appétit!

Mixed Berry Crumble

Prep Time: 10 minutes | Cook Time: 16 minutes | Serves 4

- ½ cup chopped fresh strawberries
- ½ cup fresh blueberries
- ⅓ cup frozen raspberries
- 1 tablespoon freshly squeezed lemon juice
- 1 tablespoon honey
- ⅔ cup whole-wheat pastry flour (see Tip)
- 3 tablespoons packed brown sugar
- 2 tablespoons unsalted butter, melted

1. In a 6-by-2-inch pan, combine the strawberries, blueberries, and raspberries. Drizzle with the lemon juice and honey.
2. In a small bowl, mix the pastry flour and brown sugar.
3. Stir in the butter and mix until crumbly. Sprinkle this mixture over the fruit.
4. Bake for 11 to 16 minutes, or until the fruit is tender and bubbly and the topping is golden brown. Serve warm.

Favorite Fudge Cake

Prep Time: 5 minutes | Cook Time: 20 minutes | Serves 5

- 1/2 cup butter, melted
- 1 cup turbinado sugar
- 3 eggs
- 1 teaspoon vanilla extract
- 1/4 teaspoon salt
- 1/4 teaspoon ground cloves
- 1/2 teaspoon ground cinnamon
- 1/2 cup all-purpose flour
- 1/4 cup almond flour
- 5 ounces chocolate chips

1. Start by preheating your Air Fryer to 340 degrees F. Now, spritz the sides and bottom of a baking pan with a nonstick cooking spray.
2. In a mixing bowl, beat the butter and sugar until fluffy. Next, fold in the eggs and beat again until well combined.
3. After that, add in the remaining ingredients. Mix until everything is well combined.
4. Bake in the preheated Air Fryer for 20 minutes. Enjoy!

Old-Fashioned Pumpkin Cake
Prep Time: 7 minutes | Cook Time: 15 minutes | Serves 2

- 1/3 cup pumpkin puree
- 1/2 cup peanut butter
- 2 eggs, beaten
- 1 teaspoon vanilla extract
- 1/2 teaspoon pumpkin pie spice
- 1/2 teaspoon baking powder

1. Mix all the ingredients to make the batter. Pour the batter into a lightly oiled baking pan.
2. Place the pan in the Air Fryer cooking basket.
3. Bake your cake at 350 degrees F for about 13 minutes or until it is golden brown around the edges.
4. Bon appétit!

Chocolate Peanut Butter Molten Cupcakes
Prep Time: 10 minutes | Cook Time: 13 minutes | Serves 8

- Nonstick baking spray with flour
- 1⅓ cups chocolate cake mix (from 15-ounce box)
- 1 egg
- 1 egg yolk
- ¼ cup safflower oil
- ¼ cup hot water
- ⅓ cup sour cream
- 3 tablespoons peanut butter
- 1 tablespoon powdered sugar

1. Double up 16 foil muffin cups to make 8 cups. Spray each lightly with nonstick spray; set aside.
2. In a medium bowl, combine the cake mix, egg, egg yolk, safflower oil, water, and sour cream, and beat until combined.
3. In a small bowl, combine the peanut butter and powdered sugar and mix well. Form this mixture into 8 balls.
4. Spoon about ¼ cup of the chocolate batter into each muffin cup and top with a peanut butter ball. Spoon remaining batter on top of the peanut butter balls to cover them.
5. Arrange the cups in the air fryer basket, leaving some space between each. Bake for 10 to 13 minutes or until the tops look dry and set.
6. Let the cupcakes cool for about 10 minutes, then serve warm.

Chocolate Cheesecake
Prep Time: 60 minutes | Cook Time: 0 minutes | Serves 4

- 4 oz cream cheese
- ½ oz heavy cream
- 1 tsp Sugar Glycerite
- 1 tsp Splenda
- 1 oz Enjoy Life mini chocolate chips

1. Combine all the ingredients except the chocolate to a thick consistency.
2. Fold in the chocolate chips.
3. Refrigerate in serving cups.
4. Serve!

Crusty
Prep Time: 60 minutes | Cook Time: 0 minutes | Serves 3

- 2 cups flour
- 4 tsp melted butter
- 2 large eggs
- ½ tsp salt

1. Mix together the flour and butter.
2. Add in the eggs and salt and combine well to form a dough ball.
3. Place the dough between two pieces of parchment paper. Roll out to 10" by 16" and ¼ inch thick.
4. Serve!

Appendix 1 Measurement Conversion Chart

Volume Equivalents (Dry)

US STANDARD	METRIC (APPROXIMATE)
1/8 teaspoon	0.5 mL
1/4 teaspoon	1 mL
1/2 teaspoon	2 mL
3/4 teaspoon	4 mL
1 teaspoon	5 mL
1 tablespoon	15 mL
1/4 cup	59 mL
1/2 cup	118 mL
3/4 cup	177 mL
1 cup	235 mL
2 cups	475 mL
3 cups	700 mL
4 cups	1 L

Volume Equivalents (Liquid)

US STANDARD	US STANDARD (OUNCES)	METRIC (APPROXIMATE)
2 tablespoons	1 fl.oz.	30 mL
1/4 cup	2 fl.oz.	60 mL
1/2 cup	4 fl.oz.	120 mL
1 cup	8 fl.oz.	240 mL
1 1/2 cup	12 fl.oz.	355 mL
2 cups or 1 pint	16 fl.oz.	475 mL
4 cups or 1 quart	32 fl.oz.	1 L
1 gallon	128 fl.oz.	4 L

Temperatures Equivalents

FAHRENHEIT(F)	CELSIUS(C) APPROXIMATE)
225 °F	107 °C
250 °F	120 ° °C
275 °F	135 °C
300 °F	150 °C
325 °F	160 °C
350 °F	180 °C
375 °F	190 °C
400 °F	205 °C
425 °F	220 °C
450 °F	235 °C
475 °F	245 °C
500 °F	260 °C

Weight Equivalents

US STANDARD	METRIC (APPROXIMATE)
1 ounce	28 g
2 ounces	57 g
5 ounces	142 g
10 ounces	284 g
15 ounces	425 g
16 ounces (1 pound)	455 g
1.5 pounds	680 g
2 pounds	907 g

Appendix 2 The Dirty Dozen and Clean Fifteen

The Environmental Working Group (EWG) is a nonprofit, nonpartisan organization dedicated to protecting human health and the environment Its mission is to empower people to live healthier lives in a healthier environment. This organization publishes an annual list of the twelve kinds of produce, in sequence, that have the highest amount of pesticide residue-the Dirty Dozen-as well as a list of the fifteen kinds ofproduce that have the least amount of pesticide residue-the Clean Fifteen.

THE DIRTY DOZEN	
The 2016 Dirty Dozen includes the following produce. These are considered among the year's most important produce to buy organic:	
Strawberries	Spinach
Apples	Tomatoes
Nectarines	Bell peppers
Peaches	Cherry tomatoes
Celery	Cucumbers
Grapes	Kale/collard greens
Cherries	Hot peppers

The Dirty Dozen list contains two additional itemskale/collard greens and hot peppers-because they tend to contain trace levels of highly hazardous pesticides.

THE CLEAN FIFTEEN	
The least critical to buy organically are the Clean Fifteen list. The following are on the 2016 list:	
Avocados	Papayas
Corn	Kiw
Pineapples	Eggplant
Cabbage	Honeydew
Sweet peas	Grapefruit
Onions	Cantaloupe
Asparagus	Cauliflower
Mangos	

Some of the sweet corn sold in the United States are made from genetically engineered (GE) seedstock. Buy organic varieties of these crops to avoid GE produce.

Appendix 3 Index

KARI B. ROSEBERRY

Printed in Great Britain
by Amazon

19210234R00045